Life

with my

Wife

The Memoir of an Imperfect Man

by

Roger Stoner

To Donna,
"Perfection is"
Over-rated.

Roger Stoner

Published by: WANATA Publishing
                Peterson, Iowa

ISBN: 978-1507738153
Library of Congress Control Number: 2015931911

Copyright © 2010 Roger Stoner

All rights reserved. No part of this book may be reproduced or transmitted in any form or by any means, electronic or mechanical, including photo-copying, recording, or by an information storage and retrieval system, without permission in writing from the publisher.

Second Printing February 2015

For Jane

INTRODUCTION

I first met my wife as 6:15 p.m. on Saturday, April 6, 1974. You may think it odd that after all of these years I remember the exact time, day and date that I met her. But really, it is no big deal. I remember it like it was yesterday. You see, I have a terrific memory when it comes to life-altering events.

My date with her was to be the third "blind date" I had ever been on. She was my friend's, wife's friend. Since my first two blind dates hadn't worked out all that well, I was less than confident that this date was going to succeed. Blind date number one had been with a "really nice girl" who was a friend of a friend. She outweighed me by thirty pounds, chain-smoked menthol cigarettes, and walked like the Marlboro Man. She was also "really disappointed" when she found out I didn't smoke. Blind date number two, who was a "really, *really* nice girl," and the friend of a friend of a friend, was all of four feet three inches tall and loved all of God's creatures, even the ants and sparrows. She just didn't understand how people could kill animals. She also didn't eat meat. So, she wasn't too thrilled when I told her that I liked to hunt deer and . . . eat them, too.

So it was without great expectation that I pulled into Blind Date number three's farm place. It didn't help my outlook much when I noticed that there were several vehicles parked in the driveway. (What? Was this girl finally going on a date reason enough for her family to throw a party?) Pushing aside my trepidation I pulled my 1972 blue Toyota Corona around the turn-around and parked for a fast get away. As I walked up to the door, a good-looking young girl with long brown hair, beautiful eyes, and a dazzling smile stepped out to greet me. (I figured it was Blind Date number three's good looking little sister sent out to lure me into the trap.) "Hi, I'm Jane." she said, taking my hand.

JANE—that was Blind Date #3's name! Relief flooded over me and the jokester in me wanted to say, "Hi, I'm Tarzan," but as my eyes drifted down, to her long, flowing hair that cascaded well below her shoulders and hung tantalizingly over the mounds of her bosom, I was tongue-tied. My eyes locked on her beautiful, very young face, and swallowing deeply, I managed to mumble my name. From previous experience, blind dates just didn't look this good. Something had to be wrong.

Smiling a friendly smile, she led me into the house. As we stepped into the kitchen, her three older brothers and her father stood in a line to greet me. Warning bells began ringing in the back of my head as each man shook my hand with a firm grip that telegraphed a silent message of the terrible things that could happen should I act in any manner other than an honorable one, while dating their little "Janey."

"Relax," she leaned close and whispered in my ear. "They're only here because it's my mom's birthday."

She already had the uncanny ability to read my mind. She seemed to know what I was thinking before I'd even thought it. It was a talent she would use against me many times in our future to baffle, confuse and just generally piss me off. But I didn't know that at the time, and besides, I was captivated by her beauty, charmed by her cool demeanor, and fascinated by the way she looked in the snug yellow sweater she was wearing. I was focused on that night and not worrying much about what might happen in the future.

We were married on December 20th, of that same year. I was 22 years old and working in a factory and she had turned 18 on September 2nd and was still a senior in high school. I know what you're thinking, but no, by the grace of God (and modern pharmaceuticals) we didn't *have* to get married. We got married before she was out of high school because she wanted to get married in December, not June and, well, by that time in our relationship, I was pretty much going along with whatever she wanted. My only stipulation was that she get her Dad's blessing for a December wedding (without involving me!) and that she promise to finish high school. Her Dad was easy. She had been wrapping him around her little finger for years.

After the wedding we enjoyed a two-day honeymoon in beautiful downtown Worthington, Minnesota. I don't really know if downtown Worthington is beautiful or not because we hardly left our motel room. Aside from the obvious reason newlyweds spend most of their honeymoon ensconced in their room, we had a couple of other very good excuses. The thermometer had dropped to thirty-four degrees below zero and the snow was ass-deep to a tall Native American. Adding to the need for an abbreviated honeymoon agenda was the fact that my car had broken down a week before our wedding. I had to use the money I'd saved for our honeymoon to pay for a valve job before I could get my car back so we had something to drive on a honeymoon. Luckily, we did receive just enough cash in wedding gifts to pay our motel bill. There wasn't enough for any fine dining though. So we pretty much just stayed in the motel room and feasted on nearly frozen pizza, delivered to our room by a shivering young man who didn't even get a tip. But we still had a good time.

She kept her promise to finish high school and we began our life together. We ditched the pharmaceuticals and God blessed us with a son and a daughter, born two and one-half years apart.

In 1989, our hometown newspaper was about to go out of business. With two growing kids, it had become apparent that we could use some extra income, in addition to my factory job. Jokingly, I suggested that if we bought the paper, I could write the news and she could run the office. To my surprise, when I came home from work a couple of days later, she told me that she had contacted the owners and brokered a deal. On July 1, 1989 we were in the newspaper business!

For fifteen and one half years we published the Peterson Patriot each and every week. I wrote most of the news, covered the sporting events of our local school and wrote my column, *Roger's Remarks*. The column soon became very popular with our readers, many of whom commented that they looked forward to reading my *Remarks* each week. Coming up with the material for a column every week was challenging to say the least, but many of those column ideas were inspired by the common ordinary life experiences of a man with a wife and two kids.

I think that part of the reason *Roger's Remarks* was so well received by my readership is because the events I described each week were not particular to just me. Most of the readers, both men and women, identified with certain aspects of my columns because of similar happenings in their own lives. *Life With My Wife (The Memoir of an Imperfect Man)* is the unabridged selection of *Roger's Remarks* as they were written, before being edited for language suitable for publication in a family newspaper, between July 1, 1989 and December 31, 2004.

CONTENTS

Introduction

PART ONE

PART TWO

PART THREE

PART ONE

A FINELY-TUNED ATHELETE

Did I mention that my wife took me shopping last Friday, the Day After Thanksgiving? It is the day that kicks off the Christmas shopping season and is the busiest shopping day of the year!

My wife waits for that day, like I wait for opening day of deer season. She can't wait to get out there and throw elbows with her competition. As for me, I like it about as much as I'd like having the dentist pull my favorite tooth by mistake and then have to go back in again to pull the one with the abscessed cavity that he originally intended to pull and then billing me for both procedures!. So every year, I swear, up and down, that I'm not going shopping on the Day after Thanksgiving. And this year when I said I wasn't going I *thought* I really meant it!

So when we took off shopping last Friday morning, I had to wonder exactly how it was that I was going shopping, when I was pretty sure I didn't want to go. I can remember saying, *"I'm not going with you!"* over and over again, when ever the subject came up.

The funny thing is, the wife says she doesn't even want me to go shopping with her. She says she gets tired of all the whining and crying and would be better off taking a two year old along. But there is something about the Day after Thanksgiving that seems to trigger this inherent need in her soul to drag my tired ass along and make me help in making Christmas gift decisions - a talent I do not have.

It wouldn't be so bad if we could do just what the stated goal for the day is—find Christmas presents and buy them—but she and I have differing opinions about how this goal is accomplished. I think that the holiday shopper should consider the wants and the needs of the person or persons they are shopping for, go into the store, find the items you have decided may be appropriate, buy them and get the hell out of there before the thundering herd of holiday shoppers tramples you to death!

My wife has a *completely* different plan. She thinks it is better to walk through all of the stores, and see everything that every store has to offer. While doing this, you make your decisions as to what you want to buy for each person that you want to buy for and then, and only then, you go back in and find the objects you desire to buy.

I used to play high school football. I played on the line and know what it is like to be elbowed, kicked, smacked upside the head, poked in the ribs, stomped in the stomach, busted in the chops and kneed in the family jewels. And I have to say that oddly enough, even though I enjoyed the experience at the time, I harbor no such inclinations at this stage of my life.

There is something about the Day After Thanksgiving shopping that I just don't understand. My wife never experienced athletic competition in high school and I always thought she was kind of a pacifist who didn't like competitive sports. Wrong! High School just didn't offer the right kind of contact sport. It appears that the sport of SHOPPING is more to her liking. I compare my wife's demeanor on the Day After Thanksgiving to that of a football player on Sunday afternoon! You should see her! As she enters the stores, her eyes grow a little wide and she starts breathing deeply through her nose. She holds her head high and is unusually alert, watching for her competition to try an end run or shoot up the middle while trying to slide past her. She can scoot around an island of junk for sale like a half-back and dive straight ahead into a pileup of women shoppers blocking the aisle and break through into the clear like a full-blown running back.

She can move through a crowd of mean spirited shoppers faster than a wide receiver can run a post pattern. She can intercept the last item on the shelf, snatching it from the grasp of the multitudes of other desperate shoppers, slicker than a pre-safety. She can bull her way into crowd at a *Blue Light Special* and grab the prize she desires just like a quarterback sneaking to gain that last, all important yard!

So I really think that the whole reason she wants me to come along shopping on this Day of Days is so that she can show off her athletic skills, much like a football player wants his family and friends to see him play. But I already know all about her skills on the shopping field. I've watched in awe as she has wended her way, bobbing first one way then the other, through the flying elbows, swinging hips, and the occasional flying purse of crazed shoppers for many Christmases now.

Frankly, I'm a little like the parents of young men who play football. I'm worried about possible injuries she might receive while playing the game, but realize that I have to give her the chance to shine. She, like the young men who want to play the game, deserves to have her moment in the sun. And I guess that she deserves to have her skills witnessed by a loved one.

So there are really two reasons I ended up going shopping with my wife on the Day After Thanksgiving again this year: to watch a finely-tuned athlete at the top of her game show her stuff, and, as my wife so deftly suggested, "I suppose you're going to write about this in your column and tell everybody about how much I like to shop *again*."

Yep, I've got to keep my readers posted! (And then too, she did promise me a pizza if I came along!)

THE DIFFERENCE BETWEEN MEN AND WOMEN

My wife's superior skills in the buying game are nearly legendary. She is not just well known to the sales clerks in most of the discount and retail stores in the surrounding area, she is almost famous. She knows most of them by sight and many of them by name. Many is the time, she has poked me in the ribs and said, "Look, there's Betty."

"Betty?" I answer. "Betty who?"

"Betty from K-Mart."

Or she'll say. "Look, there's Debra."

"Debra who?"

"Debra from Wal-Mart.

Sometimes, when she's on a roll, throughout the course of the day it can be like, "Look there's Lacy, Bobbi, Lindsey, Carol, Stacy, Cindy, Carla, Delores. . . etc."

And I'm just as ignorant as ever, "Lacy, Bobbi, Lindsey, Carol, Stacy, Cindy, Carla, Delores, Sandy, Brenda, Billie, Andrea, Samantha . . . etc., who?" (I added a few, just to be a smart ass.)

"You remember her. She works in K-Mart, Wal-Mart, the bread store, the dollar store, Dairy Queen, the garden center, the lumber yard, grocery store, sporting goods store, JC Penney, or the place where they sell mufflers for underwater golf carts. She's the one who used to develop pictures at the one-hour photo place. I haven't seen her in years."

And you know what? They all seem to know her too, even the ones who retired years ago and are just out there shopping themselves.

It's not only the sales clerks and employees of the different places who recognize my wife. I can't tell you how many times complete strangers walk up to her when she is in any store within a thirty mile radius of here, and ask her where they can find something like candle wicking or lamp shades decorated with dragonflies, or lavender scented toiletries, or nightcrawler bedding. They've seen her in these stores so often, *they think she works there!*

The beauty of it is, she knows where things are in most of those stores better than the people who work there do. And she is always very kind and courteous and helpful to people looking for particular items. Many times, they don't even have to ask her. She overhears someone complaining because they can't find whatever it is that they need and she walks over, tells them where what they are looking for is located, how much it costs, and gives them a push in the right direction.

What I'm saying is that she is good at what she does. She not only knows where to look for things, she knows what they should cost and where to go for the lowest price and the best deal.

She is a bit naive, at times though. She seems to believe the rhetoric these shopping-Meccas spout in their advertising. I think she actually believes that they really do want you to get the lowest price and the best deal. And when she runs across something that just doesn't seem right, she feels obligated to let them know, so they can fix it.

The other day we were in one of those stores and she decided that we needed some new flannel sheets. So she picked some out and then dragged me over to look them over. I was in kind of a hurry and agreed with the first sheets she showed me, immediately. But no, we had to go through them all and compare each and every set of sheets before she was satisfied that *we* were agreed. Personally, I couldn't care less if the sheets I sleep on have Cardinals and Chickadees or Black Bears and Moose or Iris and Daffodils on them. As usual, after we looked through the entire pile, *we* finally agreed that the set she picked out first were the sheets *we* wanted.

Then, when we finally got to go over and check-out, she brought up the fact that there was a big SALE sign hanging over the sheets, but there didn't seem to be any sheets with a marked down price. She informed the check-out girl of this and the girl immediately called her supervisor. The supervisor paged for someone in the Bedding Dept.

My wife told them that she didn't think the sheets were on sale, but that there was a SALE sign hanging over them. The Bedding Person couldn't find any of the sheets that were on SALE.

My wife said she understood that, but just wanted them to know that they had a SALE sign hanging over the sheets (which might confuse less experienced shoppers than she).

The supervisor informed my wife again that her sheets *were not on* SALE.

Once again my wife explained that she knew that, and wasn't trying to get a SALE price. She just wanted them to *know* that they had a SALE sign hanging over the sheets, which, by the way, were *not* on SALE!

Did I mention that I was in kind of a hurry?

This time, it was the check-out girl's turn. She stated once again that the sheets weren't on sale. My wife stated once again that she *knew* that and only wanted them to *know* that they had a SALE sign hanging *over* them (which might confuse less experienced shoppers than she).

I was still in a hurry. (And so were the twenty-five people who had lined up behind us while the discussion about the not on sale sheets developed. None of them had sheets.)

The check-out girl finally said that the SALE sign my wife was referring to meant only that the sheets were *for* sale and not necessarily that they were *on* sale.

Finally, the wife paid the bill and we went out to put our new sheets in the truck.

"You know," my wife said to me, "I think they just put that SALE sign up to trick people into buying those sheets without checking to see what the SALE price was. And I bet they sell a lot of them to people who think they are getting a good deal even though they're not on sale!"

"Bastards!" I cried indignantly. "To think these friendly stores and the friendly people who work in them would actually try to fool their customers into thinking that they are getting a good deal, just to make a sale?" Then with mock anger and annoyance, I added, "If they are going to pull that crap, I'm gonna stop shopping here and I think you should too!"

This just got me an angry glare. I guess she just doesn't appreciate sarcasm?

IT'S THE THOUGHT THAT SHOULD COUNT

Well, if you hadn't noticed, counting today, there is only two days till Christmas. And if you haven't finished up your Christmas shopping yet, you better kick it into high gear and get going! Let's see, you've got the rest of today, and most of tomorrow, which would be Christmas Eve. I'm not too sure how late the stores will be open on Christmas Eve, so you better drop everything and get out there today. If it's night time, *"don't worry about it,"* some of those stores never close.

You can go to an all night grocery store and buy some food gifts. Buy the wife some sardines, crackers & cheese, a bag of beer nuts and a twelve pack of beer. Or (if you're afraid she won't share) maybe you could go to a department store and buy her an iron and ironing board. Or maybe a nice vacuum cleaner, a mixer, a new fry pan or maybe something more personal like. . . a five-speed blender! They're great for when you want her to make a malt for you!

Yeah, I used to get my wife some really good gifts: batteries for the TV remote; an aluminum handled snow shovel (that wooden handled one was just getting to be too heavy for her); a mop bucket and sponge; a stiff bristled brush for cleaning the oven with; and probably the most thoughtful—a back brace so she won't hurt her back carrying the baskets of clean clothes up from the basement.

Now that I've given you some really great gift ideas for your wife, just make sure you get out there and get her something real nice.

Remember, it's the thought that counts, so you better be thinking. And then, after you get them all bought, don't forget to wrap them up so she can be surprised when she opens them. I found out early in marriage that unwrapped presents aren't nearly as well received. (Especially if she sees them before the kids are all there to serve as witnesses.)

I used to get my mom to wrap my wife's gifts, or I'd hire somebody at the store to do it. But I got tired of all the smirks and derogatory comments about my gifts selections. (My mom really surprised me.) So in recent years, I've have taken up gift wrapping myself.

In fact, I stayed up late the other night wrapping Christmas presents. I'm not a very good wrapper. The packages I wrap usually end up looking remarkably similar to something our cats drag back to the house after digging through the garbage in search of the ever illusive *essence du sardine* can. I'm not saying that my presents smell like rotten fish, they just look like they probably should.

But, with enough paper and scotch tape I usually can get the presents covered enough that their recipients can't guess what they are until after they drag them out from under the tree. And since the essence of surprise is very important to my Christmas giving experience I do my best to effectively camouflage the gifts I'm wrapping to give. Consequently, my wife complains that I use *too much* paper and *way too much* tape. I don't know where she gets that? As far as I'm concerned, you can't use *too much* tape! The more tape the merrier! That's my credo!

Recently, I found out that our children, when they were young and still living at home, actually opened their gifts to see what they were getting as soon as they were put under the tree and their mother and I were conveniently away at work. Then they re-wrapped them and simply had to recreate a look of extreme surprise and happiness on their faces on Christmas Eve when we opened our gifts. The wife and I were none-the-wiser. Ha ha! Big joke on us!

I must insert here that the presents that the kids opened and then re-wrapped, were presents their mother wrapped. I know this because when you use as much tape as I use, it practically takes a blow torch to open them. And I didn't smell any scorched scotch tape around the house. Maybe some *essence du sardine*, but that was just because the cats had been in the garbage again.

The wife is always worried that we'll run out of tape, before she gets her presents wrapped. So I almost always get the lecture about conserving the tape. And you know me, I've always responded well to a good lecture. This year, I'm considering using duct tape to wrap one of her gifts. I mean, literally, wrapping one of her gifts in duct tape. No paper, just *duct tape!!!*

At least if I did that, it might be interesting to watch her open the gift. You see, for the past several years for some reason, she has found it necessary to strongly advise me in my gift selection ideas. So she knows what most of her gifts are, because she picks them out. (What do you think she drags my sorry butt around shopping all the time for - to tutor me in what would be an appreciated and acceptable gift selection.)

She opens her gifts with a knowing smile, says thank you . . . And that is it! That's no fun at all! There is no excitement! There is no intrigue! There are no eyes shining with inquisitiveness! There is no excited anticipatory shortness of breath! There is no wonder *at what in the world could possibly be in that incredibly ugly package!*

She already knows.

At least if I wrapped her presents up in about three or four layers of pure, unadulterated duct tape, it might be kind of fun watching her whittle her way through it to find out which of the gifts that she pointed out, I bought. She can even borrow my pocket knife, but then, it is pretty dull and is probably no match for the duct tape.

So here's to a Merry Christmas; peace on earth and good will toward men, and a sharp pocket knife to help make them both be possible!

THAT MAKES A LOT OF SCENTS

Have you seen that commercial on television that ends with the guy asking, "What have you got in your wallet?" It is a credit card commercial and of course, he's trying to sell you on the idea that his credit card company is better than the rest. Well, I'm not trying to sell you anything but I'd like to ask, "What kind of soap have you got in your soap dish?"

Odd that I should ask? Maybe, but the only reason I bring it up is that I'm wondering if there is anybody else who has a bar of yellowish-cream colored soap with swirls of reddish purple streaks mixed throughout it in their bathroom?

We do.

I guess that this particular bar of soap is suppose to give off the scent of raspberries, or cranberries or some such "natural odor" when you use it. I don't know about most people, but I don't really like the smell of raspberries or cranberries or whatever it is that this soap smells like. Besides, I'm the kind of guy who likes his soap to smell like, well . . . soap.

Another thing, this stuff doesn't lather. I like to take a bar of soap between my two filthy hands and rub it and scrub it around until a nice, white, lather forms. Then you know your hands are clean and you can rinse them off and dry them without unduly soiling the towel. You can scrub until your palms fall off with this creamy reddish-purple stuff, and all you get is a little reddish-purple slime with a few bubbles in it. That's not lather. And to me, it never seems like I can get that slime to wash off. I rinse my hands and dry them on a towel and it still feels like my hands are slimy.

Needless to say, I didn't pick out this particular bar of soap. If the truth were to be known, I probably wasn't even supposed to use it. The wife didn't say so in so many words, but I think that maybe this particular bar of soap was *just for looks!*

But don't tell her I said that, because, like I said—she never said that in so many words. What she said was:

"Isn't that bar of soap pretty? Don't you just love the way it smells?"

I guess I should have taken the hint right then and there that the raspberry/cranberry swirl soap really wasn't for *general use*. General use meaning . . . me. I think it was really more for company to see, and use, if they were to happen to be in our bathroom and feel inclined to wash their hands with soap that doesn't lather.

This is not an entirely new concept around our house either. I remember a time or two when there were these special, pretty little towels that were not for *general use* either. (That would be me again.) They were only hung out when company was coming.

The problem was that sometimes, those special, pretty little towels didn't always get taken back down and put out of sight before I came along and needed to dry my hands (usually with the oily residue left from the fancy-smelling, pretty soap still on them) and I'd soil the towels in a way which couldn't be washed out and therefore, ruined my day.

I couldn't help that I had to go to the bathroom right in the middle of changing the oil in my pickup. How was I to know that that creepy smelling soap wasn't going to cut the grime and then wasn't going to rinse entirely off before I wiped them on the fancy towels?

That good old green soap that is full of grit and low on slime would have. It might have left your hands all dried out, rough and red by the time you were finished scrubbing them off, but at least they were clean and didn't have that oily feel after you dried them.

Another thing I have a small problem with is those things you can buy to plug into your outlets that periodically give off an odor to freshen the air in your house. Those sweet scented air freshening candles are hard for me to stomach too. My wife says she likes that stuff because it *smells pretty*. But I have to wonder if they aren't really some kind of a cover up?
Was there some clandestine cookie baking that took place? Has she hidden (or eaten) the evidence? (Did she need the scent of lilacs in the living room and the smell of vanilla in the kitchen to hide the aroma of freshly baked sugar, butter and flour mixed in with the unique smell of melted milk chocolate chips?)

Let me just say, for a woman who likes chocolate so well, my wife sure is into vanilla scent. Yes, we have vanilla smelling gadgets plugged into the receptacle in the kitchen. It is plugged in where the can opener is supposed to be plugged in. And we have candles that smell like vanilla in the dining room and lilacs in the living room. I have trouble with all of them. They make me sneeze! But the wife loves them.

I guess it all goes back to how opposites attract. My wife likes soap that is pretty and smells nice. I like soap that gets the job done. She likes towels that are pretty and look nice. I like towels that I can dry my hands on and not worry about how dirty they get. My wife likes to make the house smell like a candle store.

I guess I can handle the lilacs in the living room and I suppose I don't mind a little raspberry scent in the bathroom. But when it comes to the kitchen, I draw the line. I think the kitchen should smell like a kitchen. So I would rather that she use a gadget that gives off the odor of bacon and eggs in the kitchen. We have one, you know. It's called a stove.

THE PERFECT BREAKFAST

We're in the process of fixing the dining room ceiling because I left the water run in the bathroom upstairs and ruined it. So consequently, we've had to tear down a lot of plaster and replace it with sheet-rock. And the wife has been sanding the rest of the ceiling to make it smooth enough so we can spray texture back on it and make it all bumpy again. (Sand it smooth so we can make it all bumpy again? Yeah, that's what I said.)

Sunday morning I woke up about 6:30. My back was aching. I couldn't breathe because my head was all clogged up. And my hands were numb. I had been in bed for almost eight hours, which is about two hours more than I am used to. That is why my back was aching.

In the process of all this tearing out of plaster and sanding off of bumps, a lot of dust has been raised. When the sun shines in through the window, you can see minute dust particles suspended in its heat. I'm allergic to dust. That's why my head was all clogged up.

My hands were numb because they are numb every morning. I suspect it has something to do with having done what I do for a living for over thirty years. A lot of career factory workers have developed a chronic case of tendonitis in their elbows, a mild case of carpal tunnel in their wrists, and when the weather changes, all of their joints ache. Or maybe it's the early stages of arthritis. Or, since I have passed the half century mark, it may all be just a part of the aging process, like losing most of the hair on my head, or having an oversized prostate, or not being able to see without my glasses any more. So when I got up Sunday, I wasn't feeling as well rested as you would think you would feel after sleeping an extra couple of hours. In fact, I felt kind of off my feed and when I'm off my feed, there is usually only one thing that makes me feel better. I needed a good breakfast.

There was a half pound of bacon beckoning me from down in the refrigerator. So against my weight-loss counselor's advice, (Yes, I have a weight-loss counselor—a.k.a. my wife.) I decided to go down and have myself a good old fashioned, fattening and unhealthy, but delicious, fried eggs and bacon breakfast. What else can you do when bacon beckons you from the refrigerator?

Now, I like my bacon fried done, but not too crispy. And my eggs I like fried in a deep pan of bacon grease. You gently splash hot bacon grease across the top of the eggs so the white gets cooked, but the yokes stay soft. Then, I butter up a couple of slices of toast, wrap the bacon in the toast and smash it into the soft yokes and inhale both eggs, all of the bacon, and the toast in a lip smacking hurry, before any of it can get cold, or the wife comes down and starts nagging me about how unhealthy bacon is. Being able to time the cooking and eating of a perfect breakfast as described above is really an unrecognized art form.

Needless to say my breakfast Sunday deviated from "perfectness" right from the beginning. I pulled that half pound of beckoning bacon from the fridge, and with admonitions from my weight-loss counselor ringing in my memory, I cut off a quarter pound and put the rest back. I placed it in the pan and slow fried it, turning it often and everything was going good. Then I put bread in the toaster. (That's when things started going bad.) I went back to the frig and snagged a couple of eggs and set them on the counter. (That's when things started going bad.)

About that time, the toast popped up and I went to look for some butter. We keep it in the refrigerator, so I went over and opened the frig door for the *third* time of the morning and guess what - a loaf of my wife's bread (my bread is left on the table, her bread is put in the frig) decided to roll out and fall on the floor. That wouldn't have been so bad in its self, but the wrapper hadn't been securely closed and about half the loaf fell out and actually went on the floor.

Understandably, I think, this brought forth a fit of anger on my part that did probably reach a point of near hysteria. But I didn't scream and holler, I cursed under my breath, while squeezing the life out of those slices of bread that hit the floor before slam-dunking them in the garbage container.

While all of this was going on, of course, my bacon went a little beyond just being crispier than I like and passed right on into being burnt. Needless to say, when I went to fry my eggs in burnt bacon grease, it was difficult to splash the grease over the top of the eggs and I ended up breaking both yokes. I never did find the stupid butter. So my weight-loss counselor can take great solace in the fact that I ate dry toast, with charcoaled bacon so there was no fat left in it and scabby looking eggs that were somewhat less than pleasing to the palate.

"Having a little trouble down there, Dear?" my wife hollered down from upstairs as I swallowed the last bite.

What I want to know is, how did she know that I had trouble in the kitchen? She was upstairs, sound asleep and still, she knew. Maybe it's our house. I could sense the bacon beckoning me, so maybe she could sense my discomfort. Maybe there is a telepathic line from the kitchen to the bed room! Or maybe my cussing under by breath wasn't really under my breath!

REFRIGERATOR PRIVELEDGES

You know, I need to give a little credit where credit is due. My wife has been a pretty good sport over the years. I'm not just talking about when I use her as a subject of one of my columns. I'm talking about things like letting me choose which movie we go to, (she always falls asleep halfway through the opening credits anyway) and not complaining when I track snow on the carpet until she finds out I did it by stepping in it with stocking feet.

She's also pretty understanding about my needs for true contentment: hunting, fishing and playing golf. When I talk about going she says stuff like, *"Don't worry about me, I don't mind being left all alone with nothing to do."* And often, she encourages me to, *"go ahead and go if you're going to be grouchy all day if you don't."* Yeah she's a good sport.

She even used to help me pick chickens when we cleaned them back in the old days. And while I don't think she ever actually helped clean them and cut them up, she did can the old hens and wrapped and froze the fryers. She has never had a problem with me butchering the deer, wild turkey, pheasants, squirrels, rabbits and fish that I bring home from my various expeditions, as long as I do it *in the basement.* She did frown on my son's idea that the kitchen table was an ideal place to bone out one of the deer he bagged with his bow and arrow a few years back. (But he's her *little boy* so he got away with it.)

Probably the best thing my wife lets me do that a lot of wives don't let their husbands do, is keep my fish bait in the refrigerator. Yeah, in the summer time, I keep a constant container of chicken livers that I use for catfish bait in either the refrigerator-freezer or the refrigerator itself, depending upon how soon I'm going to use them. You don't want them froze solid when you use them. But you also have to be careful about leaving them unfrozen in the refrigerator for too long of a period of time. They can get a little "rank," if they sit in there too long without being used up or refrozen. (Yes, that is the voice of experience.)

Nightcrawlers are a similar problem. They are absolutely no good if you freeze them even just once. And once they've been frozen, they start to stink. Don't ever leave them in the trunk of your car overnight and then run them into the house and put them in the fridge, before you go to work in the morning. When you get home, they're still gonna be dead and the fridge isn't going to smell the best. That sort of thing tends to ruin the wife's good humor.

It took her a while to get over that. But she did, and I've been happily putting my bait in the fridge ever since. We had a slight accident the other day though. My wife had opened a can of salmon for her lunch. She didn't eat it all, so she put what was left in a plastic container and put it in the refrigerator. It was *supposed* to be her lunch the next day.

To make a long story short, I'd been up ice fishing and had accidentally torn the side of the plastic bag that I was keeping my bait in. By the time I got home, I had forgotten about the torn bait sack. So as usual, I placed the bag of bait up on the cheese saver shelf in the door of the refrigerator beside my snuff box full of diaphragm turkey calls, and that little tub of butter that stays soft even when it's refrigerated. The only problem was, the tear in the bag, gave my bait the opening they needed to escape. By noon the next day, when my wife opened the fridge intending to finish off her can of salmon, my wigglers had wiggled through the tear, dropped down a couple of shelves, and were crawling all over the lid of the container her salmon was in!

I keep the bait in the fridge to keep it from pupating. A pupa is the "non-feeding stage between the larva and adult in the metamorphosis of holometabolous insects, during which the larva typically undergoes a complete transformation within a protective cocoon," or in the instance of this particular bait, a hardened case. In other words, when this bait pupates and transforms into an adult, it becomes a fly.

So the wife accused me of putting a bag of maggots in the refrigerator and "*now we have a refrigerator full of escaped maggots!*" The container with the salmon in it, and the wigglers on it, went outside. And the good little wigglers, who had stayed at home in the bag, where they belonged. . . went outside along with their escapee brothers.

She said that *since I thought they needed to be cool, they could be cool outside.*

But it was a little too cool outside. These wigglers are a little like nightcrawlers; once you've frozen them, they're kind of hard to get on your hook. But the wife didn't care much about that.

So the next batch of wigglers I bought, I got smart and put them in a little plastic container with a lid that snaps on tight. I brought it home and stuck it up on the cheese shelf like always, right beside my turkey calls and those little tubs of butter that stays soft even when refrigerated.

Uh oh.

I sure hope the wife is wearing her glasses when she gets the butter out for her toast in the morning, because, if she should happen to accidentally grab the wrong container and open that little tub of wigglers . . . I'm probably going to get kicked out of the refrigerator again.

THE LAST SHOPPING TRIP BEFORE CHRISTMAS

I almost got out of it all-together. She wanted to make a trip to Sioux City just before Christmas just to "pick up a few last minute Christmas presents." She "just couldn't find anything for the girls" around here. So she talked me into agreeing to the trip by embedding a *Long John Silver's* craving in the back of my mind. I'm not sure how she does that - maybe it is a subliminal tactic involving flashing pictures of crispy fish fillets on our bedroom ceiling in the middle of the night. That, along with my disappointing failures at being a successful ice fisherman may have sparked an uncontrollable desire to actually eat some fish. (At *Long John Silver's* you don't have to catch them first.)

She also promised that I could take in a movie while she was shopping. So I agreed that we could go. (I just couldn't let the "girls" go without presents on Christmas). Then good old Mother Nature stepped in and it snowed and the wind blew hard enough that even my wife didn't want to try a 75 mile trip in the middle of a winter storm. So after all of the bickering and bribing, we ended up staying home.

Christmas came and, low and behold, it seems that she actually *had* found gifts for the girls which we gave them on Christmas Eve and the holiday passed merrily after all. But since I had agreed to the idea of a shopping trip *before* Christmas, just because the weather hadn't allowed us to go, was no reason for me to think I was getting out of going *after* Christmas. (That's when she really wanted to go anyway—all the Christmas items are on sale then, you know.)

To shorten this long story, I fulfilled my agreed-to obligation to take her on a shopping trip, before the end of the year. In accordance to our unwritten contractual agreement, I did get to partake in the deliciousness of *Long John Silver's* and take in a movie while she was shopping. So my wife says that I have no right to complain.

But no where in our agreement did I state on paper or verbally that just because I got to scarf down some deep fried fish and sit ten rows from the front, in a movie theater, filled with complete strangers, including a squalling baby (one row ahead and two seats to my left) and an extremely tall, burly, gentleman who obviously had never slouched in his life (sitting directly in front of me) did I give up the right to bitch about the shopping trip in this forum or any other that I should choose to discuss it in.

First, I've never seen such a crowded mess as that mall was Saturday. I walked from Target which is on one end of the mall, to Sears, on the other end and it took me over a half hour! And I was hustling! I was in a hurry see, because I didn't want to miss my movie, but it didn't start for almost an hour. So I figured I had plenty of time to check out the tools at Sears before I went to the show.

I left Target at a brisk walk. I will admit that I never ran the 100 yard dash in twelve seconds or anything close, but I can move right along when it means missing the previews of coming attractions if I dawdle. Unfortunately, there were no less than a gazillion people in the mall on the last Saturday of the year. There must have been a Christmas Sale Enthusiasts Convention in town and most of them were *slow moving shoppers!*

I think they ought to have traffic cops in the malls within three weeks (before and after) of Christmas, Valentine's Day, Easter and my wife's birthday. There should be a "fast lane" down the middle of each side and there should be NO MOPING ALONG & GAWKING AROUND signs placed every twenty feet and ABSOLUTELY NO HOLDING HANDS & WEAVING BACK & FORTH signs every ten feet or so.

I tell you I had a heck of a time making it to Sears. And by the time I got there, after dodging from one side of the aisle to the other side and dancing around all of the dawdling shoppers and couples joined at the hip, I had to turn around and head back to the theater just to be there in time to line up for my movie, without even seeing a tool!

There was a huge crowd in line at the movie theatre too! I think it was made up mostly of those of us who had been dragged to the mall against our will, by the Christmas Sale Enthusiasts conventioneers. I went to see Tom Hanks in "Cast Away." It is a very popular movie and the line to get in was long. That explains my choice of seats. When I finally got in, there were only a few single seats toward the front that were not taken.

The good news is that I will probably recover the hearing in my left ear. I expect that once I get back to work in the relative quiet of a factory setting, the high pitched wavering baby squall will dissipate, and I'll be back to hearing the steady low-pitched hum in that ear, that I am accustomed to. I'm also confident that the pain in my neck, that I got from leaning to my right and tipping my head far enough to see around that guy in front of me, will slowly slide back down between my shoulder blades where it belongs. It may take a little longer for me to heal up from the knee-jerk reaction of the big lady sitting to my right when my tired neck allowed my right ear to accidentally brush her abundantly endowed bosom.

I should be able to chew solid food again in a couple of weeks.

So really, I'm not complaining because I'd just about rather be stripped naked, coated with honey and stuffed down an ant hill than follow my wife around the mall for an afternoon of shopping. So a little hardship in the theater is really not that big of a deal.

BEGINNER'S LUCK

I am probably the world's worst shopper! I don't know how to do it. I don't know how to start or how to finish. And I don't know how to do the in-between parts either. What's probably worse it that I don't even want to know how to shop. I'd rather spend my time at my favorite fishing hole or on the golf course than in the mall.

Some people may think that I am pretty narrow-minded when it comes to the subject of shopping. I think they are unfair when they say that about me. After all, what do they think I got married for? Just to have someone to cook and clean for me? To make my meals? To provide companionship in both my young age and old age?

Well sure, all of those things are nice, but one other thing that is possibly even more important, is having someone who knows how to shop for you. I am fortunate in that the little woman I chose to betroth is not only pretty good in the companionship department; she is practically a professional shopper! She knows what things should cost and is pretty good at spotting a bargain.

Although I do think that she occasionally has lapses of "onsaleitis." That is to say that if the retailer puts a "SALE" sign by it, she is definitely going to look it over and consider buying it, even if she doesn't really need it. (But don't tell her I said that. It could make for an unhappy household, if you know what I mean.) Usually, when we go shopping, I need only drop her off at one end of the mall, and go plank my behind in a movie theater for a couple of hours and let her take care of the shopping. She usually does so flawlessly, finding articles of clothing for each member of our family.

But she let me down the other day.

After discovering that I have just about either outgrown or worn out most of my decent work clothes, it was decided that I needed to purchase some. Unfortunately, she said I had to come along and *try on* the clothes before we bought them. If there is one thing I hate worse than shopping for clothes, it is trying them on at the store before I buy them.

I could tell right away, this wasn't going to be fun. First, there was the shock of finding out that I don't fit into standard size clothes anymore, and have to buy the larger sizes. They cost at least two bucks a pair more. Honest to God, I thought I still wore jeans with a 38 inch waist.

My wife got a good laugh out of that one.

So after standing there enduring her snickering for a while, I scooped up three sizes of Wrangler jeans and headed for the fitting room in somewhat of a huff. I'm a big boy. I can pick out, try on and buy my own damn clothes. *I don't need her.*

I would like to meet the S.O.B. who designed those fitting rooms. He obviously didn't have customers who weigh close to an eighth of a ton in mind when he drew up the plans for those claustrophobic cubicles. When I bent over to remove my shoes, I bumped my head on the door and it went rattle, rattle. So I turned around and bent over to pull my old jeans off and bumped the door with my butt and it went rattle, rattle again. While trying on the three pairs of jeans, I must have bumped the door a couple of thousand times. This caused a lot of annoying rattling.

Rattle-rattle-rattlerattle rattlerattlerattle . . .

I came out of there feeling more than a little rattled! But I had triumphed! I knew which jeans I wanted!

But before I could get too cocky, the wife directed me to pick out a couple of Xtra, Xtra large work shirts. While I was picking out a couple of XXL shirts, the wife was attracted to a "SALE" table (kinda like a moth to a bright light), and she left me unchaperoned for a couple of minutes. What can I say? Once I get started spending money, I find it hard to stop. I decided to get some shoes.

I like to follow my Dad's advice when it comes to buying shoes. He always said that he wore size 10½ but 11's felt so good he bought size 12s. So, I skipped to the chase and went for a size 12 right away. I tried on the left shoe. (I always try on the left shoe.) It fit great so I didn't try on the right one. It has always been my experience that if the left one fits, the right one will too. Besides, they had them tied together with a short piece of elastic string and not only did I figure I'd look kind of funny tripping around the store in a pair of shoes that were tied together, I thought it was probably illegal to remove the elastic string hooking the shoes together before you bought them. Kind of like those little tags on mattresses that say DO NOT REMOVE UNDER PENALTY OF LAW!

So I was feeling pretty good about myself. I had two new pairs of jeans, two new shirts and a nice new pair of shoes. My wife had interfered with the jeans, making me try on those big ones instead of my size 38's. And then, instead of the "Large" size shirts, I used to buy because they showed my muscles, she insisted on the XXL size. (She must figure they'll shrink or something.) But at least I did pick out my own shoes without her telling me which ones to buy. So I was feeling pretty good about the job of shopping I had done.

In fact, I felt pretty proud of myself all the way home. However, when I got home and put my new purchases on, the oversized jeans were a perfect fit and the XXL shirts fit just the way I like them to. But there was a slight problem with the shoes. The left one fit great, but the right one felt pretty tight.

Upon a closer inspection, I found that the left one was a size 12, just as it should have been. But the right one was only a size 10. Now I don't know how that could happen when they are in a size 12 box and are tied together with a piece of elastic rope. But it did. I'm pretty disappointed in my wife for letting me get out of there without trying both of those shoes on.

You'd think she'd know better, wouldn't you?

TEENY-WEENIE BEANIES

My wife, the Collector, has started yet another collection. According to her, this collection could be the *most valuable* yet! What is it? Gold coins? Precious stones? Baseball cards?

Naw. She said she's collecting *valuable* stuff this time—Teeny Weenie Beanies! There are only twelve of the little buggers. All she has to do to get them is go to a McDonald's restaurant, buy a food item and pay an extra $1.69 (*plus tax)* per Teeny Weenie Beanie. I figured McDonalds would probably issue a different Teeny Weenie Beanie each week and spread it out over about twelve weeks, which would satisfy her collection addiction for most of the summer.

I figured that there wouldn't be a lot of interest in these Teeny Weenie Beanies. I figured she would just drop by the local McDonalds once a week, indulge in a Fillet-O-Fish sandwich (that's her favorite McDonald's sandwich), fries and a soft drink, and that would be the end of that. Twelve weeks later—collection completed—end of story. And best of all, I figured that I wouldn't have to become involved.

You know what? I figured wrong.

This Teeny Weenie Beanie thing has turned out to be kind of a pain in the padded part of my backside. It all started out with her asking me if I was interested in accompanying her to McDonalds to eat supper and pick up the first Teeny Weenie of the series. I figured, why not. I was hungry and I hadn't had a Big Mac for a long time. I figured it wouldn't take very long to grab a quick sandwich and be on my merry way.

Did I mention that sometimes I have a propensity to figure things wrong?

I had no idea there would be so many crazy people interested in those stupid little bags of beans. We stood in line for 45 minutes before we got to order a Fillet-O-Fish, and a Big Mac. Then we waited another 15 minutes for them to toss the food on a tray and hand it out to us. So that was about an hour in line and let me tell ya, when you got your chance to order, you didn't want to stutter, you wanted to spit it out. And woe to the poor Dude who had stood there so long he forgot what he wanted!

Teeny Weenie Beanie collectors can be vicious!

43

Guess what? McDonalds isn't releasing a different Teeny Weenie Beanie each week. They are releasing a different one as soon as they run out of the previous one. And they are going so fast that so far, the Collector has had to go to a McDonalds every day (twice one day), just to insure that she gets them all. She's getting so sick of Fillet-O-Fish sandwiches that she's turns a little green around the gills at the mere mention of McDonalds.

But she's a real pro. She'll sacrifice her body, not to mention her sanity, for the cause. So there's only one real problem inhibiting her chances at collecting all twelve of these incredibly popular bags of beans. I'm that problem. I wasn't even willing to eat at McDonalds more than once a week, before that crowd of pushing, shoving, elbowing, and screaming, Teeny Weenie Beanie Collectors took over the place.

I don't want to come off as some kind of a sissy, but risking bruised kidneys from an irate gray-haired old lady collector behind me in line, who wants to be in front of me, or an elbow shot to the family jewels from a midget sized collector who thinks I'm trying to push ahead of her, is not my idea of a good time. And now I'm in trouble with the Collector who counts. We had to go to Sioux Falls for an appointment with a doctor on Friday last week. While there, the Collector pointed out the local McDonalds and seeing as how I would have had to turn left across traffic that reached to the horizon and how I had cars reaching to the opposite horizon behind me, I *refused to stop!*

"I figure you can get them back home." I said.

I did tell you how I occasionally figure things wrong, didn't I?

Keeping with my patented Roger Stoner Bad Luck, since I didn't stop she missed out on two, I said *TWO* of the Teeny Weenie Beanies. Why two? I don't know. We only missed one lousy day. But consequently, I have what may be called a disappointed Collector on my hands.

So anybody out there who happens to have an extra *Claude the Crab* or *Stretchy the Ostrich* Teeny Weenie Beanie, I'm in the market for them. But I must warn you, I'm a hard bargainer and will not be ripped off! So don't try to take advantage of a bad situation. I'm not desperate or anything. If I don't find these two illusive bags o' beans, the Collector in my house will get over it . . . eventually.

A CLOSE CALL

Last weekend I took my wife to Atlantic, Iowa so that she could attend the Iowa Coca Cola Collectors convention. My wife is not a professional Coca Cola collector, meaning that she doesn't collect the stuff to try to sell it again for a profit. She just collects it for . . . hell I don't know why she wants the stuff. I just don't understand the attraction. Why does anybody want to collect items with the words *Coca Cola* written on them? I have trouble understanding the whole concept of collecting anything, let alone Coca Cola memorabilia. I drink the product and like it for its taste, not for the container. My wife, who loves the Coca Cola collectibles, drinks Pepsi. Go figure.

So, as you may have gathered, I'm not too excited about my wife's Coca Cola collection and you may be wondering why I agreed to take her to the convention. Good question. Maybe I just wanted to be nice. (Or maybe I just wanted to be able to eat my meals in the future, without hiring a food taster.)

I got dressed first in the morning (as usual) and was all ready to go when my wife, standing there, still in her underwear held up a gray T-shirt with "Pepsi" printed on the front and joked about wearing a Pepsi shirt to a Coke convention. I said I didn't care what she wore, just so long as she hurried up. After what seemed like hours had passed, she showed up downstairs wearing a bright red T-shirt that had "Coca Cola" printed in gold across the front.

That is when I found out that I really wasn't ready to go. It seems that I had put on a plum colored T-shirt when I got dressed and the wife informed me that "everyone knows" that plum and red clash.

"We can't be seen walking around the convention in shirts that clash."

She tossed me a gray T-shirt to put on and rather than argue, I just put it on without even looking at it.

We made the long trip down there (It took about 2½ hours) and walked through the doors into this large hall crowded with Coca Cola collecting fanatics, just after noon. My wife was so excited! She started going through the hall table by table, item by item by item by item by . . .

I looked stuff over pretty closely too. There were bottles and cans and pins and pictures and trays and openers and . . . it must have taken me all of seven or eight whole minutes to go through that entire convention hall and get thoroughly bored to death. So I went back to the car and tuned in the Iowa - Illinois football game.

Iowa was having a pretty easy time of it and by half time, I found myself getting kind of sleepy and I started drifting . . . back into the convention hall. I was looking for my wife, hoping she was ready to go. I mean, she must have been in there for most of a couple of hours anyway! But of course, with the size crowd that was in there, I couldn't find her right away, so I started walking around looking for her. To be honest, I guess I couldn't help letting some of the disdain I feel for these fanatical collectors show. Before I knew what I was doing, I was asking questions like:

"Why would anybody want to buy this rusty old scratched up tray you have on display here for $125?"

"Why should I give you $5 for that divot fixer, just because it has Coca Cola written on it, when I can get a divot fixer at any golf course for free?"

"Why would I want to buy this 7 ounce bottle of Coke from you for $300 when I can go buy a 20 ounce bottle right over there in that vending machine for a buck and a quarter? *Are you stupid or what?*"

The next thing I knew, I had grabbed a bottle opener laying on the next table over, popped the cap off that $300 bottle of Coke and guzzled it right down. I thought the guy was going to pop a main vein!

"*What did you do that for?*" he screamed. "That was a priceless bottle. It was bottled in 1992 and has American Airlines written on the side. Only people who contributed $2500 or more to the AA Museum got one of those bottles!"

He was really pissed!

"Sounds like somebody really got took back in 1992 then." I sneered.

All of a sudden I noticed a crowd was gathering.

"What's going on Bernie?" I heard a big bearded fellow shout from behind me.

"This guy with the damn Pepsi shirt on just drank my American Airlines bottle and he doesn't even act like he's very sorry about it. He doesn't seem to understand the *whole concept* of collecting Coca Cola memorabilia!" Bernie blubbered.

I think the guy was actually ready to cry!

I could hear a growing rumble as the crowd grew even bigger. But I think they were going to disperse until some derogatory shouts got them all fired up again!

"What an ass-hole!"

"What's the matter with that guy?"

"Doesn't he understand how valuable that bottle was, *before it was opened?*"

"He doesn't care a bit about collecting and he's an insensitive pig too!" came a familiar voice shouted by a woman in the middle of the crowd. "And I should know!" the voice added.

I saw a blurry red T-shirt with gold Coca Cola lettering and from that general direction I heard the same voice shout, "Let's hang the bastard!"

Several hands grabbed me and tried to wrestle me to the ground. I fought back like the former high school football player that I am, but to no avail. There were just too many of the fanatics for me to handle. They pulled me over and stood me on an antique Coca Cola pop bottle case that was standing on end. They tied a rope to a rafter and put it around my neck. Then this familiar woman, wearing a red T-shirt with Coca Cola printed in gold across her chest, kicked the antique case out from under me and . . .

". . . and Timmy Dwight was hit hard and fumbled the ball as he crossed the goal line," the announcer was saying as I awoke from my dream in a cold sweat.

It was a long afternoon at the convention.

MY BUDDY JACK

My good ol' buddy Jack had kind of a problem. He always had this habit of going out and running around all night. Which wouldn't have been so bad except for the fact that more nights than not, he'd get into a fight and get himself all bunged up. I tried talking to him about it. I told him it was kind of dumb to go out and get into a fight every night, especially if he was going to lose every fight every night. But he wouldn't listen to me. It seems that there was more to the story than just Jack and some other guy getting together to bump heads. It seems that there was more than likely a female involved. It's the same old story. It's been happening since time immemorial. You get a couple of young studs out there on the prowl and some pretty, young, sexy thing walks between them and you have World War III in the making.

"You don't have to fight over every sweet young thing that happens to cross your path." I tried to tell him that it really wasn't necessary to get into a fight every night. "There are a lot of fish in the sea." But he wouldn't listen and it got to be pretty bad.

Oh, he didn't go out every night. It depended on how rough of a day he'd had. And I guess he didn't actually get beat up every time he went out for the evening. But when he did, he wasn't a pretty sight in the morning. You see, my buddy Jack is no quitter. If he got into it with some guy, he was there for the duration. He wasn't going to back off or back down. He wouldn't be bluffed and he wouldn't be buffaloed. He's as game as they come. Unfortunately, he was more of a lover than a fighter. I remember once he showed up at my front door early in the morning. He was battered and bloody. He looked like he had run into a real buzz saw that night.

"I sure hope she was worth it." I quipped as I opened the door. He just gave me a lop-sided grin as he limped past me and collapsed on our couch. He just spent the day lying around our house and never said a word. Of course, I think he liked the way my wife fussed over him. She scolded him for fighting. But then she fed him a meal and patched up his cuts and bruises and pretty much pampered the heck out of him. It almost made me want to go out and get into a good knock-down drag out, just for the sympathy I *might* get. I say *might* because I remember the two or three times I've been in small scuffles during the years of our marriage, and never once did I hear anything sympathetic come out of my wife's mouth for me. I guess I just never got hurt badly enough.

The way it would work for me is that if I went and picked a fight with Mike Tyson and he bit my ear off, she'd just say I should have known better than to pick a fight with "Iron Mike." But as for my buddy Jack, it was as if he was a hero, even though he probably got beat. I say he probably got beat because he never has admitted losing any of the fights he has been in. (One of those kind of guys.) The part that really disgusted me was that Jack never seemed to learn his lesson. He'd go out, get all bunged up and have to lay around for a couple of days recuperating before he could be counted on to take care of himself. And the bad part is that he started making a habit of spending those days of recuperation laying on MY couch with MY wife fussing over him. I don't mind telling you that no matter how good of an old buddy someone is, when they start getting more attention from your wife than you get yourself, it can become a serious situation.

Finally one day, there was the straw that broke the camel's back. Jack came to our house after what must have been a pretty successful night of carousing around. He had a smart-aleck grin on his face and a bounce in his step I hadn't seen for a while. It looked like he might have been in a fight, but must have won. He strutted into the house, walked right past me, brushed up against the wife on his way into the dining room, where he leaned up against the wall and peed in the corner!

That was pretty much the end of the wife making a fuss over him. In fact, she took Jack up for a little visit with the doctor the next day. And he ended up staying there for a couple of days. When he came back, it took a few days of recuperation before he was ready to go back out on the town. And then just the other night we saw Jack walking around our back yard.

My wife couldn't help but notice that he looked a little confused. I told her that after his operation, Jack probably *was* a little confused. After all, being neutered probably didn't change him from wanting to be out there looking for something every night, but it might have made him *forget what it was he was looking for.*

Yep, I said *neutered*. A little word of advice: if you want to stay on the good side of my wife, don't pee in the corner of her dining room . . . no matter how hard you've been hitting the catnip! In case any of you may not have caught on yet, my ol' buddy Jack *was* our big ol' black and white Tom cat. But I guess now, you'd have to say he's just our big ol' black and white cat.

LOST BEAR—ALL POINTS BULLETIN

Be on the alert for a pink, fuzzy bear—missing since sometime last week. It is thought the bear may have tried to commit *bear-acide* in the latter part of the week as he was found by a casual passerby, neck deep in the toilet bowl of the newly remodeled bathroom in a Peterson residence. A casual passerby became somewhat of a local hero, when he plucked the unfortunate bear from the porcelain cooled waters and tossed him into the family bathtub somewhere around 5 a.m. He quickly reported the incident to the fuzzy pink bear's owner, who mumbled something about a "Stupid Cat" and rolled over and went back to sleep.

But in the morning, the fuzzy pink bear's distraught owner (the casual passerby's wife) was quick to lay the blame for the bear's near death experience on a fine, upstanding family cat with a slight history of *bear mauling*. The cat, however, denies any knowledge of the fuzzy pink bear's dip in the stool, and is sticking to the 5th Amendment, a tactic he also used when questioned about the apparent decapitation of a fuzzy brown bear at an earlier date.

The cat has been seen hanging out with the fuzzy brown bear's head. However since the bear's body seems to be missing, there is no *corpus delicti* and, therefore, there is no real proof that a crime has been committed. (It is possible that the fuzzy brown bear pulled its own head off and then ran off and got lost because without a head it couldn't see where it was going and who knows which box of junk in the basement it could be hiding under?)

Meanwhile, a possible break in the near drowning of the fuzzy pink bear case, has run into a dead end. A furry blue rabbit was found hiding behind the door in the same newly remodeled bathroom, where the fuzzy pink bear took a dive into the cooling commode water. The furry blue rabbit has under gone extensive questioning by the distraught bear owner. But the blue bunny, a possible witness to any crime that may have taken place in the newly remodeled bathroom, has remained mum, and hasn't spilled any beans about the fuzzy pink bear and what may or may not have happened to it.

The furry blue bunny rabbit has also refused to answer any questions about how it traversed from its home downstairs in the dining room, near the locked bear cabinet, to the newly remodeled bathroom on the second floor?

The distraught bear owner, (a.k.a., The Collector) is adamant that the black and white family cat has something to do with the sudden disappearance of the soaking wet pink bear since it was gone before she got up in the morning. She labeled the disappearance as "evidence tampering" but has no real proof as the blue bunny is still refusing to talk. The fuzzy pink bear owner thinks the bunny has been intimidated to silence by the cat. But she's having a hard time convincing the bathroom remodeling, fuzzy pink bear-saving hero of the house that his black and white cat had anything to do with the bears or the traveling rabbit.

The angry beanie bear owner has even gone so far as to recruit the bitchy calico cat that lives in the house too, as a witness against the black and white cat. But the calico cat's testimony is tainted by her extreme hatred for the black and white cat rendering any of the Calico's testimony as false accusations.

"So where is my fuzzy pink bear?" the bear owner wants to know.

Who knows? Maybe the fuzzy pink bear just walked off on his own. Maybe he searched out a tall mountain where he could just sit and contemplate his own *pinkness*? Maybe he was angry because he wasn't locked away safe and sound with all of the other bears in the collection and had to sit alone atop the tank of the porcelain throne in the newly remodeled bathroom? Maybe we'll never know. So far, the black and white cat and the furry blue rabbit aren't talking and you can't believe a word that lying calico says. Until the fuzzy pink bear shows up, it will all remain a mystery.

The fuzzy pink bear owner is accusing the black and white cat of "*just trying to get even*" for being neutered.

A possibly true accusation, but an unprovable one too.

A HERO'S COMMENTS

There was an attempted drowning at our house the other night. I know that a guy probably shouldn't admit to something like that, especially not in a published account that is sent from coast to coast. But I have nothing to hide. In fact, I consider myself to be sort of a hero in this deal. While I'm not one who usually blows my own horn, I feel compelled to, in this case, because if I don't, nobody else is going to tell you about it.

Now don't get me wrong. I'm not looking for a lot of credit here. I don't want anyone patting me on the back or saying things like "atta boy Rog!" I'm not telling you this just to make you think I'm a nice guy. But this is a story that needs to be told and if I come up looking like a hero of sorts, or at least a good guy, in the process, well, I can't help that.

The scene of the near drowning just happens to be in our newly remodeled bathroom. I tore out all of the old stuff and replaced everything in the room. I put in a new bathtub, a new stool and a new sink. I don't mean to make it sound like I did it all by myself. I did put new tile in the ceiling by myself, but it took four men with the aid of a team of chiropractors to carry the new heavy bastard of a cast iron bathtub upstairs. I finally had to call in a semi-pro to fix my leaky plumbing job. And then, giving credit where credit is due, my wife laid the linoleum, the carpet and papered the walls, which in effect, covered up all of my mistakes. If you don't believe me, *just ask her.*

However, none of that has anything to do with my recent act of heroism. It was just last Saturday morning. I had stayed up late Friday night, drinking diet cola and watching a smutty action/adventure movie on television. Consequently, I had a nature call at about 5:03 a.m., which happens to me just about every morning around 5:03. Since that morning, like every other morning except for Sunday mornings, I had to get up at 6:00 a.m. to go to work, my only thought was to hurry up and get back to bed so I could sleep for almost another hour before rising for the day.

But something just sort of felt a little. . . I don't know . . . . different, I guess. Usually, I just stumble into the bathroom, answer the call, flush, and stumble back to bed. I don't turn on any lights. I don't look around. I don't check things out. The truth is, I'm hardly even awake.

I've been making this early morning trek every morning for as long as I can remember. It is just something I do. Kind of like, staying up late drinking diet colas and watching television shows that I don't really want to see. It's just something I do. I can't explain either of them for sure. I often wonder if drinking the diet colas late at night has anything to do with having nature call before I'm ready to wake up in the morning. I don't think so because I tried drinking regular colas instead and it still happened.

Next I'm going to try just drinking water. Maybe it's the cola itself. I'll figure it out.

For some reason, on that particular morning, even though I was still dead tired and still half asleep, something told me there was something wrong in that bathroom. I tried to shake the sleep from my mind. I usually do my business in the dark, but for some reason that morning I turned on the bathroom light. Even though I couldn't see very well due to the sudden brightness of the lights, I had the undeniable feeling that something was out of place. Some one thing was wrong in that room. And then, I spotted it! The pink bear which usually sits on the stool tank wasn't where he (or she, I have problems sexing those bears) was supposed to be! And then I saw it.

My wife's fuzzy pink beanie bear was sitting neck deep in the bowl of the stool. (Luckily, I saw it *before* I answered nature's call.) It was all but gone and if I had just used the facility in the dark, and flushed - who knows what might have happened? (Well, I know what would have happened. That stupid bear would have clogged up my new stool. Water would have run all over the floor and I'd have had to call in more than a semi-pro plumber to fix it.)

I snatched that bear from the gaping cold bowl of death, grabbing it right by the head (the only dry part left), held it over the bowl to let it drain, until I couldn't stand the sound of water tinkling in the stool any longer, and I threw the bear in the tub. Then I finished my business and went back to bed.

After the wife awoke and was told the story, she wanted to blame our big black and white cat, Jack, who has a bear hunting history. I did my best to convince her it had more than likely been a case of *bear suicide* (The pink bear, tired of being teased by all of the brown, black, gray, red, green, and blue bears she has around the house, had just decided to end it all.) I almost had her believing it, but then ol' Jack walked into the room

56

carrying the head of a fuzzy brown bear that has been missing its head for quite some time. (I had almost convinced her that that particular bear had lost its head because of a gambling debt it had refused to pay to some of the other bears.)

But ol' Jack is just too stupid to help himself out. He loves to play with the wife's bear collection as much as she loves to just have them sitting around. If she leaves one of them unlocked and unguarded, he takes it down and plays with it. He holds it with his front paws, and kicks hell out of it with his back feet. He throws it the air. He picks it up by the scruff of the neck and shakes the living shit out of it, like he would a dead rat. (If he wasn't scared of dead rats, that is.)

That's what I always thought stuffed bears were for - to play with. But my wife thinks that dragging them to the basement to hide, ripping their heads off, and now, drowning them in the stool is more than just a little innocent fun. She thinks Jack has a personal vendetta against her bears and said she *"might as well quit collecting them if he is just going to ruin them."*

God I love that cat.

THE FAVOR

My wife asked me to do her a favor the other day. On the surface, it seems like a harmless enough request. I mean, people do other people favors all of the time. It is a common, and I should think, natural occurrence, especially between two people who have been married for over twenty years.

This wasn't the first time she has asked me to perform this particular favor for her. In fact, she has asked me to do it several times over the years. I usually try to get out of this rather distasteful task, but from time to time, I have gone ahead and carried out my duty as a husband with dignified aplomb. But after what happened on the last occasion that I relented . . . I may have to decline doing her the favor ever again.

The thing about this favor is that it is an act that husbands are often asked to do, which their wives feel is only a simple consideration that should be performed as repayment for similar favors they have done for their husbands. As for me, it is a task I really don't mind doing in the privacy of our own home, or when the two of us are alone together in a fairly secluded spot because I certainly don't want to get caught doing it.

But she has a knack for coaxing me into doing it for her and it seems like every time she bats her eyes and says "please," we're in a public place like a busy parking lot and I have to tell you, if someone sees me doing it, it is just plain embarrassing! She knows how much I hate doing it but that doesn't stop her from asking this favor of me.

Consider this scenario:

We're walking down the main throughway of a crowded shopping mall. There are dozens, maybe hundreds of people flowing along with us, with an equal amount walking the opposite direction, causing a great jumble of humanity. In other words, a very crowded public place. Approximately half, the male half, of this mass of citizenry is bored out of their minds, and are just looking for something, anything, to catch their interest and entertain them. That is when my wife snuggles up close to my side and takes hold of my arm as we wind our way through the crowd. She reaches up, squeezing my biceps, pulling me close, indicating that she wants to whisper something in my ear. I lean over so I can better hear her soft murmur against the background noise generated by a shopping mall full of people.

As my ear nears her lingering lips, I hear a slight intake of her breath, (a small gasp at the firmness of my upper arm???) and I can feel her warm breath as it plays tantalizingly across my cheek. Then I hear, in the soft voice she always uses when trying to gain great favor with me, "Hold my purse for me for a second, will you? I think I've got something in my shoe."

Now this is not a great deed. This is not a favor that requires a huge amount of strength, dexterity, or even a lot of work, but it does require a lot of intestinal fortitude. Why, you ask? Why does holding my wife's purse in a building full of smirking shop-a-holics require an extreme amount of intestinal fortitude?

Well, it is because at that very instant, when she holds the purse out to me, and the straps slip into my hand, an unnatural phenomenon occurs. As her hands lose contact with the purse straps, it is as if she completely disappears from the very earth we live on! It is like she never existed and no one can see this woman kneeling at my side to take off her shoe and remove the offending what-ever-it-was that was hurting her foot.

But I'm not gone. I am right there. *Right there* in the middle of a gazillion people, half of whom are so bored that they have nothing better to keep their attention than to notice some poor bastard who has just been left holding the bag!

"See that guy? He's got a purse!"

"Look Mommy. That man has a purse!"

"Now Honey, it's not nice to stare at people, even if it is a man with a purse!"

"How come Daddy doesn't have a purse?"

"Shhhhhh! Daddy doesn't need to carry a purse."

"Where did you find that gorgeous bag?" (This came from a gentleman wearing a pastel yellow shirt and baby-blue trousers.)

My wife slipped her shoe back on, stood up with an evil grin on her face, and walked off into the crowd *without taking her purse back.*

It is amazing how the crowd seemed to spread out. Only a brief instant before, we were enmeshed in an elbow-to-elbow crowd in the mall, but as soon as the wife slipped into the crowd, it was as if I was in the center of a clear forest meadow, standing alone, holding a purse.

A man with a purse, *The Main Attraction*—on center stage!

I'm sure that many of you still don't understand what the big deal is. I'm a big guy. I ought to be able to handle a few smirks from the crowd. So you still don't understand why, from now on, I will hesitate to do this one little, harmless favor when she asks me to?

Well, someday when I have time, I'll get together with you and explain in detail the difference between merely *holding* your wife's purse for a couple of minutes and actually *carrying* your wife's purse while walking through a crowded shopping mall.

MORE FAVORS

Did you ever see that commercial on television, where the guy comes out of a doctor's examination room with a relieved look on his face and says, "The doctor says I have hemorrhoids, but I don't need surgery. All I need is a tube of Such & Such cream." (Not the real product name.)

Now before anyone gets too repulsed by the subject of hemorrhoids, hemorrhoids, the painful, itchy, repugnant creatures that they are, are not actually my subject. My subject is the Such & Such cream, or the obtaining of said cream.

I mean as soon as you enter an apothecary and ask for the Such & Such cream, the apothecary guy, (some people call them druggists) knows you got hemorrhoids! He doesn't actually smile, but you can see a certain light in his eyes that is hard to read. It isn't exactly a look of amusement. Maybe it isn't even a light, maybe it is a mask, hiding what . . . pity?

Possibly. But only if he's ever had hemorrhoids himself. Then, to top it off, if it is a busy apothecary, (and how many drugstores have you been in lately that aren't busy?) there are a bunch of people standing around watching as the guy leads you to the place they keep the Such & Such cream. Maybe they have never experienced the horrors of hemorrhoids or maybe they are just insensitive louts. But they all know what Such & Such cream is and what it is used for. So they do their share of smiling and tittering. Some even giggle, some might even laugh. A stony glare from you and the druggist usually stops them from downright guffawing.

By this time, the embarrassment has turned your face beet red and you begin to wonder if maybe surgery wouldn't have been much easier. In short, not only the hemorrhoids themselves, but also buying the remedy for them, are both very real pains in the ass.

Now to the real subject I wanted to talk about. Have you ever been asked by your wife, during that *special* phase in the cycles of her life, (the one that comes around every month . . . hopefully) to drop by the store and pick up a certain feminine hygiene product? Well, you talk about a tough situation. You can hardly turn her down. I mean she's probably in a very, shall we say, *delicate* mood. Any hesitation on your part to do this "one

63

little thing" may cause the fires of hell to come raining down on the rest of your day and continue through most of a week. But talk about embarrassing. I mean most guys, (me included) don't even know where, "the store" keeps those particular kinds of feminine hygiene products. And you know that there is a better than average chance that you are going to end up having to ask for help finding them.

So the first thing you do is go to a new place, a big place, where there is lots of people who work there . . . lots of people who don't know you and will probably never see you again. But when you get there, you are a little hesitant to ask anybody's help because the only people, who happen to be working at the time, happen to be pretty, young girls, who hardly look old enough to even know what you are asking for. Not that it would be much easier to ask a young male employee for the location of the product, because they probably wouldn't know what the hell you were talking about. But at least with another guy, you could shrug and look sheepish and whine about having to run errands for "the old lady" to keep the peace. (Not that I'd ever call the light of my life, "the old lady")

So, anyway, since you just can't find *anybody* to help you, you decide to go on a search and seizure mission and find the damn things yourself. You take a cart, ('cause you don't want to end up at the checkout counter with only that one item) and casually stroll up and down the aisles picking up a few things here and there. By the time you find what it is you went there for, (hint—they're usually in the aisle with the diapers) you have a cart full stuff you don't need and it ends up costing you your beer money.

Which brings us full circle. In short . . . having to go buy feminine hygiene products for your wife is a similar sensation to having hemorrhoids.

A TAXING TIME

Last week was the one single most dreaded week of the year for me. Since, once again, we ignored our tax preparer's advice about keeping our financial records updated throughout the year, the wife and I spent most of our non-sleeping hours gathering together all of the information we need for filing our income taxes. It was about as much fun as having your wisdom teeth removed without the benefit of anesthesia.

We always wait until the last minute, with tax day looming, to start. It's always a mad scramble to get everything ready to go, but this year something happened to make things even madder. Before it was all over, I was mad. The wife was mad. The kids were mad. Our dog was mad. We have one fish in the aquarium—he was mad. About the only ones not openly affected by income tax time are our cats. And that is only because they are so stuck up and uppity that they seem like they are mad all of the time anyway.

Probably the most chilling aspect of this year's episode was when we thought we had misplaced my W-2 forms. The wife stated unequivocally that she had placed them in the tax booklet and put the booklet in the box that we use to keep tax stuff in, and stuck the box on the floor in the corner beside the hutch.

"If they are not there, somebody must have taken them out and misplaced them!" she added looking at me. That was her way of accusing me of getting the tax booklet out while snooping around and losing the W-2s in the process. I was entirely sure that I had placed the sacred W-2s in her hands when I brought them home from work and had not seen them since and told her so. That was my way of accusing her of being a careless "Keeper of all Things Important" and expressing my extreme disappointment in her performance of this office.

At that time, the loss of the W-2s was an unexplainable phenomenon. But being reluctant to blame such things on aliens or ghosts, we did the only natural next best thing. We blamed it on the kids. Of course the kids, being totally innocent bystanders, were not too thrilled about being labeled as the losers of the W-2s. The whole thing was an enigma. One day the

W-2s were there in the booklet, in the box, in the corner, and the next day they were gone!

Now I realize that it is probably not the end of the survival of the human race if you lose your W-2s, but it is rather irritating, not to mention that getting them replaced would likely be a big pain in the ass! It's almost like losing your billfold. It's not the cash money I would lose that bothers me. Let's face it, five wrinkled dollar bills is nothing to get too sentimental about. The real pain is replacing your driver's license, credit cards (if you have any that aren't maxed-out), insurance identification card and pictures of your loved ones.

I imagine it is possible to get duplicates of your W-2s, but losing them on the night before you go to have your taxes prepared, is a little like losing your helmet on the way to play in the Super Bowl. You might as well just stay home. I must say though that I am rather proud of the way we handled this crisis. There really wasn't too much hollering and screaming. We kept it to a low roar. The accusations that I wrote about earlier were only uttered in frustration not real anger. And we never really pressured the kids, other than just asking them if they had seen any important looking papers lying around. (I might have been a little rough on the gold fish though. I don't like to be ignored and he just kept swimming to the opposite side of the tank without paying much attention to my interrogation.)

But after we had looked in every conceivable place we could have put them and it was evident that they were definitely lost, we did only what comes natural to us in moments of impending disaster . . . we went out to eat. Then when we came home with full stomachs and calmer minds, we tore up the room again and finally found the missing W-2 forms hiding out in the box in the corner by the hutch in the Iowa Income Tax booklet.

"I know I put them in the Federal Tax booklet," the Keeper of all Things Important stated defensively, adding, "Somebody must have moved them."

Maybe it was aliens.

PART TWO

REMOTE WARS

A television remote control can be a wonderful thing. It can also be a curse.

For years, I fought even the idea of having a television with remote control capabilities. The thought that one could change the channels, and the volume, without ever rising off one's dead ass, seemed sort of lazy. After all, it seemed to me, if you are going to sit around on your butt and watch television all day or all night, the least you could do is get up to change channels or turn the volume up or down.

Okay, I'll come off my high horse and come clean. At that time, I couldn't afford to buy a new television with remote control capabilities. Add to that the fact that I had two little remote controls just out of diapers, running around the house. With a little coaching, they got pretty good at turning the channel changing knob until one of the three channels our antennae pulled in had a show on that I wanted to watch. I am not claiming that this was a flawless system. Since they had a short attention span, the kids had their own version of "channel surfing." The problem was that they weren't interested in the programs being shown, only the commercials. It was tough when one of my little remote controls suddenly decided they were bored with the episode of *Gunsmoke* that I was watching and decided to turn the TV to a very interesting ad featuring the latest advances in feminine hygiene products.

Consequently, by the time cable television, with the capability of receiving multiple channels, was made available in our town, I was ready for a TV with a real remote control and I bought a new "cable ready" TV!

Also, by that time, my little remote controls had grown to an age where the suggestion that one or the other of them actually get up from their comfortable lounging to change the station for old dad, was more than likely to spark an argument as to whose turn it was. This finally led to open rebellion about *why do we always* have to do it?

So at first, the remote control was the great peace maker. Yeah, for about two or three days, life was good. I could change from channel to channel without bothering anyone. And I could even immediately lower the volume if the phone rang or if a particularly annoying commercial came on with blaring clarity or whenever my wife entered the room.

But then one day, the remote must have grown hands and knees because it crawled off and came up missing. Nobody knew where it was. We looked for days without finding it until it was finally discovered that it had run upstairs and laid itself down on the table by the phone. Next it was found lounging on the counter in the kitchen. Then it was hiding on the back porch, between the couch cushions and down the side of the chair. Once it even made it as far as the basement. Over its short lifespan, it was sat on, stepped on, kicked into and dropped on the floor, or vice-versa.

It's hard to believe but that first remote we had, quit working. We tried putting new batteries in it, but it still wouldn't work. So then we went through trying to get one of those *"universal"* remotes to work on our television. They're considerably less expensive than a remote with the same brand name as your television. Did you know that you can get a single *universal* remote that will work not only for your television, but for your VCR also. In fact, if you believed the manufacturer's boast, the one we bought would control the TV, VCR, Stereo and possibly even the dishwasher. But in the real world, I couldn't even get the damn thing to turn the TV on let alone change channels or tell the VCR to record a movie for me. (We didn't have a dishwasher—maybe it would have worked on it if we did.) However, it did make a mighty fine conversation piece, laying there on the coffee table.

"Is that one of those *universal* remote controls?"

"Yep."

"Does it work?"

"Nope."

"Well . . . it looks real nice layin' there though."

"Thanks."

Through the years following, I picked up a few more televisions: one in the kitchen, one in the den, one in the basement, one in the bedroom. They all have remote controls, which, since the kids have moved out, seem to stay in a closer proximity to the TV they came with. And, they have all remained in reasonable working order, except for one.

We bought a brand new 32 inch television, VCR, and Surround Sound, all of the same brand, and a cabinet to house them in. I set it up in our living room. Included with the purchase, for only a few extra payments, was a fantastic *Extended Five Year Warranty!* It would cover anything that went wrong with the set from "bumper to bumper."

Therefore, as could be expected, the remote control for that TV began slowly going on the fritz. Oh, it would still turn the TV on and off. And it would change the channels if you pushed the buttons real hard. And the volume control sort of worked . . . if you pointed it in just the right direction and pushed hard enough and held it long enough. We tried new batteries. No dice. Even the functions that did work just kept getting worse and worse. So I told the wife to call up the place we bought the TV and tell them we need a new remote. After all, we did buy the extended warranty just for a case like this.

Well, it seems that the remote control wasn't considered to be within the "bumpers" and therefore wasn't covered under the extended warranty. So for just the price of an arm and a leg I bought a new remote. The new remote worked great the very first time I tried it. We could have thrown the old remote away. But I couldn't bring myself to just throw it away. I reasoned that it might still work as a backup if the new one should grow legs and wander off to hide from us some day.

The only problem with this idea is that now the wife sits in her chair with the old one. The reason this is a problem is that the *previous channel* button works fine and dandy on it. And since our tastes in televised entertainment are about as similar as black and white, we sometimes have what I call *"dueling remotes."*

I'll be watching something I like and close my eyes for an instant during a commercial and bang! QVC is on the screen. I touch the *previous channel* button and ESPN is back.

"I thought you were sleeping!" QVC

"Nope!" ESPN

"You sure looked like it!" QVC

"Huh-uh." ESPN

"Just let me see what Today's Special Value is." QVC

"I was watchin' the ball game!" ESPN

QVC . . . ESPN . . . QVC . . . *ESPN* . . . QVC . . . *ESPN* . . .

"I'm going upstairs and watch QVC in bed! Good night!"

My only hope is that my batteries outlast hers.

AN INCONSIDERATE JERK

Have you ever noticed how inconsiderate some people can be? It's just terrible how people can be so full of themselves and what they are doing and not even notice when they are interfering with the happiness and well being of other people. I, my very own self, was a victim of some awfully inconsiderate actions last weekend.

Let me start at the beginning. It was a cold, windy day with sleet and snow, but I had promised to take my wife shopping in Sioux City. She was a little worried about traveling that far with possibility of nasty road conditions. But like I told her, "I'm sure as hell not going to waste a *nice* day going shopping." Besides, I had been hoping to watch the Vikings/New England football game, and when I tuned in FOX, I found the Bears/Redskins game. So thinking the Vikings game wouldn't be televised, I readily agreed to take her shopping. Then, just before she was ready to leave, I turned it to NBC and there the Vikings and Patriots were! After I found my game I have to admit, that I thought about saying something about the roads really being too shitty to attempt such a trip after all. But I'm just too dog-gone fair minded for that. A deal's a deal.

She squealed a little when I tuned in the car radio and picked up the play-by-play. She hates sports, but I guess if I was considerate enough to give up watching the game to take her shopping, she could be considerate enough to let me listen to the game while we drove down there.

Right? RIGHT!

Well the roads on the way down weren't all that bad and we made it just as half-time was coming. So I dropped the wife at TARGET and promised to meet her back there in a couple or three hours. Then I made a bee-line to Sears and found the TV section and *lo and behold* practically every TV in the store was tuned to the Vikings/Patriots game! I was in heaven. I was getting to watch the game on a sixty inch, big screen TV! And I was only standing about eight feet away from it. It almost seemed like I was standing right on the sidelines!

I was getting rewarded for being a nice guy and taking my wife shopping even though the Vikings were playing. Everything was great!

Then, all of a sudden a bunch of inconsiderate people, who acted like they were shopping for a television showed up. I mean I would think that even a blind person would be able to tell that the reason I was standing in front of that big TV looking at it, was because I *wanted to see and hear* the game. But there were so many ignorant, inconsiderate people in that overcrowded store. They kept walking *between* me and the big screen which blocked my view entirely.

I learned at a very young age that it was virtually a sin to walk between a man (my father to be exact) and his television. It is just something that you don't do. It isn't like the space *between* me and the TV was the only place they could walk. It was like these jerks could see how interested I was in the game and just couldn't keep themselves from trying to block my view *right at the critical moment*! The pass would be in the air, the runner would be diving for the 1st down marker, the punter would be kicking the ball . . . it didn't matter, that is when they walked right in front of me. And nine times out of ten, they stopped and stood there looking at the TV, like *they* were the ones watching the game.

I finally figured out that this one jerk that kept walking back and forth between me and the TV was a guy who worked there. For some reason, he seemed to be bothered by the fact that I was watching one of his TVs. But he didn't have the guts to approach me. He didn't even try to sell me the TV.

In fact the sneaky little puke purposely turned a nearby stereo system to the "Eardrum Shatter" setting on the volume control. The noise coming out of it was some creepy band screaming at the top of their drug-ruined voices and it made it almost impossible to hear the play by play. Then he stood over there acting like he was trying to sell the stereo to some oriental people.

Hah! He didn't fool me. Those people couldn't even speak English. I think all they wanted was to know where the bathroom was. Now, I've never been one to be "out-inconsidered," if you know what I mean.

So I walked up to the TV, found the volume control and turned it up. Using the pretext of wanting to show the oriental couple the stereo's powerful volume, the jerk turned the stereo up. I saw his challenge and reciprocated. Stereo loud—TV louder! We kept this up until I had the TV maxed out. He thought he had me because the stereo had a little more oomph when it comes to volume and he used it and drowned out the ball game for about 20 seconds. That's how long it took me to move over to a row of 15 TVs. I turned 'em all up to the max and then did the same to another row of 20 more.

I could hear the game, baby! I taught that squirrelly little stereo-pusher not to be messin' with the football game. Hah!

The oriental people ran out of the store holding their hands over their ears, followed by the creep who was trying to sell them the stereo. Everyone else in the store (a crowd was forming) was looking in at the television section. Then some guy in a suit (I think he was some kind of a big wheel.) came running in, gave me a dirty look and turned the stereo and the TV's off . . . all of 'em.

The game wasn't quite over yet and I didn't get to see the end. How inconsiderate of him.

What a jerk!

EVER GET ANNOYED?

I do. In fact, I've been getting annoyed so often lately, that I've decided that it is time to do a little analysis and see if I can figure out why. I hope to determine if there is a geophysical reason so many things seem to annoy the hell out of me or if maybe I just like being peeved!

A person, liking to be perturbed, is not such an outlandish possibility. When you are annoyed, you're a little bit mad. You're not crazy mad, not furious or enraged, just a little bit angry. The first thing that happens to your body when you start to get mad is that your adrenal glands begin to secrete adrenaline and you feel an instant surge of energy. Thus, for a brief instant, when you first become annoyed, you feel good!

Then again, even as you are getting your adrenaline rush the annoyance is doing nasty things to your psyche. That's when your mind adjusts your body's responses to your social and physical environment. In other words, it seems like someone is playing mind games with you. No, I don't like being annoyed. It just happens and I can't seem to help it. For example, when I set an item on a table and it immediately rolls off, I don't like it. This happens to me way too often and when it does—each time it does, I immediately get ticked off! I don't like it, when a supposedly inanimate object becomes animate, and rolls off the table. And, it especially pisses me off if the item in question happens to be square or flat and it still rolls off the table like it is on wheels! I think that is the case where *geophysics* may be an applicable reason for becoming annoyed.

But there are many other things that annoy me that probably have nothing to do with physics. I get annoyed when someone starts talking to me while I'm trying to hear the television. Computers, in general, annoy me. Someone interrupting my conversation with a friend annoys me.

Telemarketers annoy me. Most music videos annoy me. Radios on golf carts annoy me. Cell phones on golf carts annoy me. Warm beer on a golf cart annoys me. My golf clubs seem to annoy me quite often too. An empty gas tank, in my truck, lawn mower, or the golf cart I'm renting, annoys me. Bright lights on a dark night annoy me. Firecrackers, even on the 4th of July, annoy me. My alarm clock annoys me every morning.

Females who demand equality, but insist on special treatment, annoy me. Rush Limbaugh, Don Imus, Jerry Springer, Jenny Jones and even Oprah Winfrey annoy me. George Carlin, even though he is dead, annoys me. Most of the people who sell things on television "infomercials" annoy me. Calling soccer football annoys the hell out of me. Sleeping through my alarm clock and getting up late annoys me. Losing my glasses, my car keys, and/or my billfold annoys me. It seems I lose all three on a regular basis and finding them all exactly where I put them shouldn't annoy me. . . but it does.

Finding the water picture in the refrigerator being empty annoys me.

Finding the ice cube trays in the freezer empty annoys me. But what annoys me the most is having my wife tell me that no one else in the house uses water from the refrigerator or ice from the freezer, and thus, realizing *who* must have put them back empty, annoys me even more.

A slow drain in the shower annoys me, as do tripping, stumbling, and falling. In a related subject, my bifocals really annoy me sometimes. You know what probably annoys me as much as anything can possibly annoy me? That damn buzzer in my pickup. It buzzes when I turn the key on before buckling my seatbelt. It buzzes if I leave the key in the ignition when I get out. It buzzes if I open my door, while the motor is running. It buzzes if I leave my headlights on after I have shut the motor off and opened the door.

Oh yes, I know that the buzzer is there to remind me to buckle my safety belt. I understand that it is there to warn me if my door is ajar while I am going down the road. I can perceive the idea behind buzzing to remind me that I have left my keys in the ignition when I get out and I am fully cognizant that the buzzer is there to warn me that I have left my lights on after shutting the motor off and leaving the vehicle.

But there are times when I don't want to buckle my safety belt. Like when I'm merely backing up to hook up to my boat trailer. When you are an untalented backer, as I can be at times, you have to jump in and out of your truck several times to see how close or how far away you are from the hitch. Buckling your safety belt each time is ridiculous and that damn buzzer gets real, *real*, *real*, annoying.

Then there was the time that I intended to leave the keys in the ignition. I was leaving my truck for my brother-in-law to use if he needed to. I left the keys in the truck with no intention of taking them out. So when I heard that eternal buzzer, I thought *"I know my keys are in there You Stupid Buzzer, I want to leave them there."*

But, when I came back six hours later, the truck was still sitting where I had left it, with the keys in the ignition *and* my headlight knob pulled to the "on" position just like I'd left it. My battery was as dead as Abe Lincoln.

Wouldn't you think they'd have a different warning sound for leaving your headlights on, than for leaving the keys in your ignition? Instead of a buzzer, there should be the sound of your wife's nagging voice saying, "Hey stupid! You left your lights on!"

INANIMATE OBJECTS AND ME

Consider the poor slob who falls asleep on the couch while watching television and wakes up, realizes that he has already seen this episode of *MASH* seventeen times before, punches the off button on the remote control, rolls to his feet and begins to negotiate his way to the stairs leading up to his bedroom in total darkness.

Did he actually sleepily stumble off course in the dark and bang his shin on the coffee table? Or when the light from the TV went off and the room was suddenly blanketed in total darkness, did that rotten bastard of a coffee table silently stretch itself over just enough to have its razor sharp corner catch the unsuspecting sleepy walker eight inches above the ankle. That is the exact location, where the shin bone protrudes the nearest to the skin surface thereby placing *most of the human body's pain sensors at the focal point of the impact.*

This painful collision throws the victim into such a painful rage that a string of uninhibited foul language flows from his very soul, decrying the birth of the very first person who discovered coffee, Juan Valdez, his donkey, and every generation of coffee pickers since that fateful moment, when coffee was first accidentally spilled into the Aztecs bathtub, making the invention of coffee tables so popular that now, even people who don't even drink coffee *have the cursed things sitting in their living rooms!*

I'm wondering if anyone else talks to inanimate objects, or am I the only one? My wife hates it when I converse with things that can't hear, see, or move, let alone respond to what I am saying. She says that it is not only senseless to call a table that I've just bumped my shin on, a filthy name; it is a little bit crazy!

"The table has no ears. It can't hear you. It has no feelings, so calling it a nasty name won't hurt it. It just makes you look silly." My wife the psychoanalyst.

I'm not a passive person. I have retaliation in my bloodline. In childhood I was taught that if someone, or something, did something to physically hurt me, to do what I could to make sure it didn't happen again. I have to tell you, cursing an inanimate object may not affect that object in the slightest, but it sure makes me feel better. And that, after all, is what I'm really after.

So, here's the problem. When I bump my shin on the coffee table, the obvious thing to do in order to make sure I never bumped my shin on it again would be to kick the rotten son-of-a-bitch into a million pieces! Right? Or maybe at least move it to a less traveled area in the house. But, in our whole big house, the *only* place for that coffee table is right there where it is sitting. Just ask the *Arranger of Furniture* at our house, if you don't believe me. According to her, I should just get used to it being there and, "*be more careful.*"

I would be more careful if I were walking along an icy sidewalk, near a busy highway where one slip might very well lead to my falling in front of a speeding semi, loaded with highly poisonous gas. Or, I would be more careful if I were walking along through a mine field, carrying a vile of highly explosive, liquid chemical that would, with the slightest jolt, blow up half the world and kill half the earth's population. Or, I would even be more careful if I were carrying an open container of potentially messy Thanksgiving Dinner scraps containing excess turkey juice not needed for the gravy, turkey skin, turkey fat, turkey bones, ham fat, ham bones, excess ham juice (also not needed for the gravy), a mixture of milk, water and lemonade, left undrunk in the glasses, and mashed potatoes & gravy, turkey & ham gristle, yams, green bean casserole, turkey dressing, scalloped corn, cranberry sauce, macaroni salad, half-eaten buns, meringue from pie, burnt pie crust, pumpkin pie filling, and anything else that was left on the plates or deemed unusable for the meal, across the kitchen, through the back porch, down the steps, around the big tree, past the garden and behind the garage to where we put the garbage. (Which is only slightly different than going over the river and through the woods to Grandmother's house.)

I would be careful doing all of that stuff! But, *being more careful* when I'm just walking through my own living room on my way to bed, empty handed and without the fate of the world or even the chance of an incredible mess if I should trip on the coffee table, just isn't in my genes.

Now, I've come to accept that the Arranger of Furniture at our house has put that coffee table in the *only* location that we could *possibly* have it. It *has* to sit where it sits. And *I know* that, I know that it is there. I also *know* that if I just *wake up* and *pay attention* to where I'm going that I probably wouldn't bump my shin on the table. I am *also aware* of the fact that no one else living in our house, has *never, ever* bumped *her* shin on the table. So I'm not really saying that the table shouldn't be sitting where it is sitting, though a health hazard to my shin it might be. All I'm saying is that when that rotten, sneaky sonofabitchin' table stretches out in the dark and bangs the bony part of my hind leg, I should be allowed to give it a serious cussing out! And, after surpassing the peak of my pain tolerance, I should be able to *threaten* it with whatever manner of retaliation that my pain-racked mind might conjure up!

After all, she already has all of the hammers locked up to protect our computer, a not-so-inanimate object, and will only let me have one on special occasions, like when I actually want to install a nail into a piece of wood. So I don't understand what the big deal is? When the table slides out and practically breaks my leg—yes, I'd like to whack it like I would a biting dog. I'd like to smack it like I would a kicking cow. I'd like to bust it into a thousand pieces (which by the way, I wouldn't need a hammer to do). But I don't.

All I ask is to be allowed to merely call it a few choice names at the top of my lungs until the pain in my shin subsides, without recrimination from the Arranger of Furniture.

I ask only this, knowing full well, that after I go to bed, the coffee table just sits there giggling evilly and waiting for next time.

A TISSUE ISSUE

To some people, facial tissue with a patented "oil-free lotion" built in is quite an invention. But I don't like it. Yeah, it might feel pretty good when you have a cold and your nose is sore from too many wipings. It might also feel soft and gentle on your face when you are removing your makeup. (That is, if you're the kind of guy who wears makeup.) I'll even grant that it may be okay to use for catching your tears when you are watching a sad movie. (Again, that is if you are the kind of guy who cries while watching sad movies.)

So I have little use for these fancy tissues because I don't wear makeup and when I cry during sad movies (and it has to be a sad movie like when Old Yeller dies), I do what any self-respecting man does: claim the tears were caused by me choking on my popcorn and get up and leave the room. All these new fangled things do is cause trouble.

What brings this all to a point is that here the other day I had dirty glasses. I was in the upstairs bathroom, so I grabbed a tissue out of the box sitting on the stool tank. Without paying much attention, I swabbed it around my lenses and threw it in the porcelain throne and flushed it. I then slipped my spectacles back on my head and I took off to go downstairs without actually looking through them and when I came to the steps, I damn nearly broke my neck.

I have no-line bifocals so looking down at an angle through the lenses can be an adventure in itself. Especially when you are looking through lenses made blurry by unknowingly using a lotioned tissue to clean them with. I misjudged where the steps to downstairs began and nearly took a tumble. Luckily, I was able to grab the banister just in time to keep from somersaulting down into the living room.

I pulled off my glasses and upon seeing how terribly blurry they were, I thought to myself, "I didn't do a very good job of cleaning them." I went back to the bathroom medicine chest and took down a little squeeze bottle of eyeglass cleaner.

You know what? It doesn't do a bit of good to use eyeglass cleaner if you are going to use a lotioned tissue to wipe it off the lenses with. I cleaned them again, and they were still just as smudged as before.

Confusion reigned!

I used two, three, four different tissues, before finally resorting to my old faithful method of cleaning my glasses: *hot water and soap*. But even that doesn't work when you're too ignorant to realize that your lenses are being made blurry by the tissue you are using to wipe them with!!!

I am not a patient man and I was just about ready to blow my cork! Those damn glasses were within mere seconds from being crushed back into the sand they were made from when the wife called up the stairs,

"Now don't be wasting all of the tissue. I bought the ones with lotion in them." Somehow, she had sensed that I was using her precious tissue. (How does she do that?)

I had used about half the box and still had messed up glasses! But suddenly, having dirty glasses wasn't the most important issue. I'd used up half the box of her very expensive lotioned tissue! That was the issue. My blood pressure began a steep rise.

I kept an eye out for the wife because I could hear her coming up the stairs as I "fluffed up" the remaining tissues in the box, hoping she wouldn't notice how depleted the box was. I quickly gathered up the pile of used tissues, determined that it was beyond being used for nose jobs, cleaning up makeup or wiping up tears, and flushed it down the toilet. I was a Boy Scout leader so I was prepared with my faithful old plunger, but luckily, it didn't clog it up. Then, I hurriedly grabbed the good old glass cleaning standby; three or four squares of toilet tissue, and started wiping the lotion off my glasses.

While I was still swabbing the toilet tissue around on the lenses of my glasses, I quickly glanced down to see if there were any tell-tale signs of the used facial tissue and was immensely glad to see that it had all went bye-bye with a single flip of the commode handle.

Everything looked to be in ship-shape and I was feeling pretty good. But, my serenity was shattered when my wife asked, as she came through the bathroom door, "How did you like the new toilet paper? I bought the lotioned kind."

AAAAAHHHHH!

SPORTS BAR

What do you think of when you hear the words, sports bar? Just the sound of it conjures up images of a dark, smoke-filled room. A bar runs the full length of it and a crowd of avid fans pushes and shoves to get near enough to order their favorite beverage or at least catch a glimpse of the baseball, football or maybe even hockey game showing on the television set. It sits high on the back wall near one end amid the half empty bottles of liquor, the cigarette dispenser and the cash register.

Usually, most of the customers are all pulling for the same team. But sometimes, their loyalties are split. Often there is some shouting and scuffling and occasionally even a fight. But still, the main focus is on the game. These people came to this bar to drink some beer and watch the game. Some come for the camaraderie of watching the game with their friends. Some come because they can't get the game where they live because it is "blacked out". Some come for the party atmosphere. And some probably come because their wives won't let them watch the game at home.

Whatever the reason, the sporting event on the television is the main calling card that brought all of these people together in that place. That is what I think of when I think of a "sports bar." There are two "sports bars" in this area that my wife and I attend on occasion. The key word here is *wife*. I said that my wife and I occasionally patronize these "sports bars."

This wouldn't be so odd, except for the fact that it is my wife who enjoys going there, not me.

Now you (especially you liberated women out there) probably wonder why I say it is odd that my wife is the one who enjoys visiting the sports bars. Well, it wouldn't be particularly odd if my wife enjoyed sports. But she doesn't. In fact, for the most part she hates sports. She gets mad when she walks into the room and sees a football game on the TV. . .

"Is that *still* on?"

"How *long* do these games last?"

"How come if *football* season is here, they're still playing *baseball*?"

"How *many* games do they play in one day anyway?"

"How come they're playing *golf* if it's football and baseball season?"

. . . is just a sampling of the questions she has asked me when I happen to be exercising my middle-aged male right to watch sports on the weekend.

So, you ask, and I can understand why you might be a little confused by all of this, "Why does your wife want to go out to a "sports bar"?

It is very simple. The "sports bars" we have here are anything but sports bars. Oh yeah, they not only have a television with a game on. They have several televisions placed strategically throughout the establishment so that every patron, no matter where they are seated can see a TV that is tuned to ESPN.

They're not dark, dingy or crowded, smoke-filled rooms. They are spacious, well lit, brightly painted and have a heck of a good menu of both food and beverage items for their customers' enjoyment. Instead of a grizzled, ex-marine bartender, they have bubbly, young waiters and waitresses who are there at your beck and call.

The food is good and not overly high-priced. I've never even witnessed someone looking cross-eyed at someone else in these sports bars, let alone getting into a fight over the game on one of the TVs. So now, I can hear you wondering out loud, "Why doesn't Roger want to go to these "sports bars" if they are so nice?

I'll tell you.

If I am going to watch a game, I want to be able to HEAR the game. I want to hear the play by play guy. I want to hear the color man make an ass out of himself trying to explain why they ran that particular play and why it did or didn't work. I want to hear every grunt, groan, agonizing wale and curse that the players make. I want to hear the *smack of the pads, the crack of the bat, and the roar of the crowd*! I want to hear it all!

But do you know what you hear while watching the game in these "sports bars?" Music. FM radio-type stuff. Rock & Roll, Country & Western, whatever they happen to be playing that day. I say either shut off the TV's and play the music or shut off the music and turn up the TVs!

Last time we visited one of these "sports bars" and I was complaining about not being able to hear what they were saying about the game on the TV I was watching while we were waiting for our orders, my wife advised me to go into the men's room. My wife had just come back to our booth from visiting the ladies' room.

"They have TVs in the bathrooms here." She said, adding "The game you're watching is on in the Ladies' Room and you can hear it in there."

So I went to the men's room but came right back out. The TV in the men's room was tuned to a station airing the afternoon soap opera, *Days of Our Lives*. They had a ball game on in the women's bathroom and a soap opera on in the men's bathroom.

Shit! I don't know if I'll ever go back to that place again!

A PIZZA EPIPHANY

Something I really need to do is lose some weight. When I bend over to tie my shoes, it takes my breath away. I get winded just scooping snow out of the end of my driveway. Sometimes I even have to lie down on the bed to button my jeans, (a trick I learned from my wife). I've been trying to discover what could have happened to that lithe, athletic body I used to have. (I used to play high school football you know.) How could I have turned from being fairly fit into the overweight blob I am now? What could have happened to change my make up from what it was to what it is?

In my searching, I've discovered lots of different reasons for having gained over fifty pounds since I graduated from high school. One reason is that I've more than doubled my age since then. And then there is genetics. I am practically a mirror image of my father. A big man—more powerful than a locomotive—sturdy as on oak—solid as a rock—who did tend to be on the heavy side.

A lot of experts like to blame the weight problem on your history. Things like, if your mother was a good cook (whose mother wasn't?) and what kind of food you grew up eating. Many of us were hooked on a high calorie, high fat, high cholesterol, and high sugar diet by our mothers, when we were too young to defend ourselves. Sure we all grew up eating those foods that have now been found to be bad for our health. Nobody knew any better then, not even the experts. Those foods taste good, so why wouldn't we eat them? My mom didn't cook any different than any of my friends' moms cooked. My friends are not all seventy pounds overweight. So I can't blame Mom.

After extensive research along with a lot of soul searching, I've come to realize that I can blame neither my history nor genetics for being overweight. In fact, there is only one person who can be held accountable for my tonnage. I have come to the conclusion that the only person I can blame for my weight problem is my wife!

It's all her fault! She's an excellent cook, with the natural ability to concoct the most delicious homemade soups, stews, and casseroles. She

91

can bake a ham or roast a turkey with the best of them. The only thing Julia Child has over on this woman is a good agent.

But it's not her good cooking I blame for my weight problem; it's *her* lack of control. She is always preaching to me how if I would eat slower, I would eat less. Consider this scenario: I've just finished up one huge helping of supper while she is still filling her own plate. I decide to go for seconds. She tries to stop me. But I feint left, then right, hit the floor, roll left, somersault right and come to my feet by the stove with hardly a bruise and without ever having dropped a crumb from my plate. She didn't stand a chance—she never played high school football. (Needless to say, our kitchen/dining area takes kind of a beating on nights she is trying to get me to diet.) So if she just had a little better control (on me) I wouldn't be so overweight.

Another reason she is to blame for my weight problem is the fact that she eats so damn slow. I, on the other hand, after having worked in a factory for over thirty years where I have about fifteen minutes to both heat and eat my meal, am somewhat quicker at eating. One reason she eats so slowly is that she actually *chews* her food instead of using the "bite-swallow-choke-and gasp for air method" I've made famous over the years.

You may wonder how the fact that she chews her food contributes to my overweightedness? Well, let me tell you. Consider this scenario: We are in a pizza joint. We've ordered a large, thin & crispy supreme. (That's one with everything on it.) I've eaten my four pieces and the wife has eaten two. I'm sitting there, *ready to leave*, (After-all, we've been there for at least twenty minutes already.), and she's only beginning to eat her second piece. So what is the natural thing to do? *Filch a piece or two of her share*, what else? I'm certainly not going to sit there and watch her chew her pizza. It might be a little more entertaining if she'd choke or gag or something once in a while, but just sitting there watching her chew is pretty boring.

That's where this eating-slow-to-eat-less thing became clear to me. Usually, I eat so fast that I have five pieces eaten before she is done with her second piece. So by eating more slowly, it would allow my wife to get her fair share of the pieces of pizza. Therefore, I would eat less pizza than I normally eat, which might help lead to a weight loss for me! But then I realized something, an epiphany if you will: Eating slowly enough to let my wife have an equal number of pieces, while maybe helping myself to lose weight, might actually cause her to *gain* weight.

How thoughtless of me!

A thoughtful husband should support his wife in all of her endeavors and it seems to me he should therefore, "take the bullet" for his wife by eating extra pizza to save her from eating all of those calories.

And I am nothing if I am not a thoughtful husband!

FANCY FOOD

My wife says I'm a picky, finicky, eater and terribly uncouth! I don't know how she figures that? Anyone who knows me knows that I like most food. Oh, I'll admit there are some foods I don't like at all, such as sweet potatoes, spinach, pea salad, beets, and those white grubs you see the Aborigines eating every time there is a *National Geographic* program about Australia on television.

But (except for those white grubs), for the most part, it can be said that I like to eat most foods that can't outrun me. I am a little picky about potato salad though. I really liked my dearly departed mother's potato salad and my wife and my sisters make good potato salad too. But I have to be really careful about taking a big plate full of the stuff if a stranger has made it. (Potato salad is hard to hide in a potted plant.)

Even though I'm sort of a meat and potatoes kind of guy I also like vegetables and am not afraid to try different things. I like Chinese food, Italian food, Mexican food and sea food. I've tried crawdads, muskrat, and common barn pigeon (cooked over an open fire). I've eaten chubs, dog fish, and carp. I'm not crazy about bear meat, but I love deer, elk and wild turkey, squirrels, rabbits, and pheasant. I would also like to try moose some day.

I've eaten wild plums and the jam made from them. I love strawberries, mulberries, peaches, oranges, grapes and most fruits and nuts both foreign and domestic.

I guess I'm telling you all of this to more or less prove that I'm not afraid to try different things and am not too hard to please. But . . . I'm not one for many fancy foods.

Having said that I should tell you that the wife and I ate at a fancy food function the other night. I could tell it was a fancy food function because my wife made me wear a white shirt and my dress pants. And with my record for spilling stuff I am eating on the belly of my shirt (no matter what color it is) I knew this had to be a very fancy function.

The meat and potatoes (the important part of the meal) were really delicious. But while partaking in the vegetable portion of the meal, I had to wonder why it is that certain foods are thrown together. Take for instance, green beans and, oh, let's just say something like, well . . . *almonds*.

I had to wonder who it was who thought up mixing almonds with green beans and calling it Green Bean Almondine? With a name like that, it has to be a French concoction! I can see it all now. It was probably back near the turn of one century or another, when a bunch of French chefs were standing around nipping on the cooking sherry bottle and trying to dream up a dish that would piss off their stuffy English enemies, in case they were ever conquered by them.

Suddenly, one of the chefs said, "Sock Le Bluer" (I can't spell in French either!) "Let us mix zee grenbens, with zee allmands. Zat weel reely peez zem off!"

I know my French is a little rusty. (That's what happens when you only take the class because the teacher is good looking.) But in my opinion, the last good idea to come out of France was the French fry!

I love green beans with a little butter, some salt, a sprinkle of pepper— and hey, give me a fork! I'm ready to chow down the green beans. And, I absolutely love almonds. Salted almonds, Smoked Almonds, Almonds just removed from the shell! I like them a lot. But there is just something about shredding them up and baking them in a pile of green beans that ruins the almond experience for me.

I even tried separating them on my plate. It didn't work!

I ate them. But I didn't like them.

While I am already complaining, (I'd hate to waste a good opportunity to bitch.) what's the deal with that red, ring- thing they always put on your plate at fancy meals? Is it a candied apple or is it a sneaky way to try to get me to eat a beet pickle?

Yeah, I'm always on the lookout for somebody trying to get me to eat beets. I don't like 'em. I wouldn't touch one of those red ring things with a ten foot pole, even if my wife does say it's *"just a spiced apple"* and *"good for you."* I sure as hell can't trust her. She's one of the people who are always trying to get me to eat beets because, "They're good for you."

Another thing those fancy cooks put on your plate is that little sprig of green stuff that looks like somebody just cut it from a weed patch and stuck it on your plate just to see how many people will actually eat it. Can't you just see those French chefs standing out in the kitchen, peeking through the crack between the swinging doors and giggling uncontrollably every time some dumb guy like me, who doesn't know any better pops the sprig o' weed in his mouth and eats it?

"Parsley" my wife called it. "It's just to add color and make the plate attractive. Don't let your imagination carry you away!"

There she goes, reading my mind again.

But hey, if you want the plate to be attractive to me, just fill it with steak, potatoes, and plain ol' green beans. If you have to bring almonds into the equation, solve my nut craving by just giving me a hand full of salted, smoked almonds to enjoy with my dessert. You can just leave off the beet ring and sprig o' weeds and I'll be a happy camper.

This is the kind of attitude that makes my wife accuse me of being uncouth. And I guess maybe I am a little *uncouth*, but at least I'm honest.

Okay, if I'm going to be honest—I lied about taking French in High School. I didn't really take it . . . she just wasn't that good looking!

TAIL LIGHTS

I'm not a car person. Never have been and never will be. I don't pay any attention to size, shape, color or make. As long as when I get in it and turn the key, it starts, that is all that really matters to me. How it looks or how I look sitting in it carries absolutely no weight with me.

I suspect that my rather lethargic enthusiasm when it comes to vehicular interest stems from the very first car I had to drive. It was a sickly salmon and white colored Pontiac Bonneville of 1959 vintage. I won't embarrass myself by trying to tell you what size engine it had, because I don't know and couldn't even make an intelligent sounding guess. I do know however, that it had a 4 barrel carburetor and plenty of power. That car would pass anything on the road . . . except for a gas station.

My dad bought the car and told me I could have it to drive on three conditions: 1) I had to put all of the gas, oil, repairs and tires on it and pay my own insurance, 2) I had to teach my mother to drive with it, and 3) if he even heard of me squealing the tires once, he'd stomp me through the cement!

I never did teach Mom to drive, but I did pour every penny I earned into keeping that behemoth running. The insurance on a teenage male took a healthy chunk right off the top of what I made working on the farm. Just the day to day replacing of things that kept running low or wearing out took the rest of my whole summer's wages. By the time I had laid out the cash for tires with tread, I sure as hell wasn't going to chance a good stomping through the concrete just so I could wear it off by squealing them.

For the amount of money it cost to keep that thing running, you'd think I put the greater share of the 80,000 odd miles that were on it . . . on it. But the beauty of it is, I was working on the farm and milking cows at the time, so I didn't really have time to go anywhere and do anything very often. What I'm saying is that I didn't run the wheels off of it and it still kept me broke.

At the end of that summer, I gave Dad his car back and went out and bought a Volkswagen bug. It was an ugly little red convertible about four years newer than the Bonneville. The big difference between the two cars was that the Pontiac would pass anything on the road except a gas station and the Bug wouldn't pass anything on the road, except for a gas station. So I suspect this experience led me to grow rather unconcerned about anything other than basic transportation.

My wife, on the other hand is a car person. She loves the shine and the glitter of a well taken care of vehicle. She is quite particular about what she drives. It has to be the right color, have the right tires and she has to feel that she looks right in it. Now maybe this sounds strange to some of us, but I think that car people, I mean people who really love vehicles, know exactly how she feels.

When we were dating, she could tell me what kind of car was ahead of us at a distance of a mile and a quarter. And this was at night. When I asked her how she knew, she said she could tell from the shape of the tail lights.

In a related subject . . . the other day when we were walking in a shopping mall, she stated that the woman walking in front of us had a certain brand of jeans on. I asked her how she could tell. She said by the shape and style of the back pockets.

That is kind of like identifying a car by its tail lights right? Well now, identifying jean brands by their tail lights might be something I could take an interest in!

ROADKILL

We were driving down the road the other afternoon and my wife, ol' eagle-eye, spotted a pheasant standing in the tall grass on the edge of the road about fifty yards ahead of us.

"Watch out for that pheasant." she warned.

"I'll watch out for the pheasant." I answered, adding, "I like pheasants. The last thing I want to do is kill one by hitting it with my pickup."

A short while later the wife spotted a flurry of activity on the edge of the road up ahead again and immediately identified it as a cat.

"Watch out for that cat." she advised.

"I'll watch out for the cat." I answered, adding, "I, unlike the popular male stereotype, *like* cats. The last thing I want to do is kill one by hitting it with my pickup. Besides, it might fly up and break out a headlight or crack my grill." (That would be just like a damn cat. They get even.)

We were on the homeward end of a road trip to Sioux Falls, South Dakota, so the afternoon was quickly turning to evening and out and out nightfall wasn't far off.

"Look out for that skunk on the road up there!" was her next warning. My wife is pretty terrified of hitting something with our vehicles. I always thought it was just because of the damage that would naturally occur and the following expenses that accumulate. Not to mention the hassle with the insurance company.

"I'll look out for the skunk." I answered calmly, adding, "I *like* skunks. The last thing I want to do is kill one with my pickup. Believe me!"

I successfully dodged around that black and white member of the aromatic cat family and hurried on toward the ever darkening eastern sky line.

"What is that up there? See it? Do you see it?"

"Yes, I see it." I answered as we bored down on an opossum, its beady little eyes and pink little nose shining in the glow of my head lights.

"Well don't hit it!"

"I won't hit it. I like good ol' possums." I said, adding, "The last thing I want to do is kill one with my pickup."

Opossums are like skunks in the way that neither of them appear to be in a hurry to get out of your way. They just sit there in the roadway and more or less dare you to run over them. Skunks, as you might understand, are more successful in this tactic as can be witnessed by the number of opossums you see "playing possum" on the edge of the road around the countryside.

But I missed him and kept the wife happy.

As we rolled on, I suddenly spotted several sets of eyes on the road ahead, but before I could even begin to touch my brakes and slow down my navigator started the warning siren from her seat on the rider's side.

"Look out, there are eyes on the road ahead!"

"I'm looking out." I answered, applying the brakes and adding, "I *like* eyes. The last thing I want to do is kill some eyes with my pickup."

The eyes belonged to a family of raccoons; Mama, Poppa, and three half-grown youngens. I slowed sufficiently enough for the whole bunch to get across the road safely. Somebody's sweet corn patch was going to take a hit tonight.

"I *like* coons." I stated after we were by them. "The last thing I want to do is kill one with my pickup."

Then it was the ultimate—the wife spotted a deer up ahead at the far reach of my headlights.

"*Look out*! There's a deer!" she screamed.

I nearly jumped out of my seat, as I slammed on my brakes and swerved, left then right and straightened out just in time to see the doe walk demurely down into the ditch.

"Don't scare me like that." I said. "I thought that deer was jumping right out in front of us." I added, "The last thing I want to do is kill a deer with my pickup. It would probably mess up my front end and do a few thousand dollars in damage. Besides, I *like* deer."

"Forget that," my wife said, "What I'm worried about is that the impact may activate the airbags and I'll get my neck broken when it hits me."

"I never thought of that. But if I put this baby in the ditch trying to dodge a deer that I might miss anyway—the same thing could conceivably happen." I answered. "I'm not blind you know. I just can't see well out of one of my eyes. The other one has perfect vision." I snapped, adding, "I appreciate the fact that you don't want me to mess up my truck, or us, by hitting animals while driving at night. I *like* animals. I *like* deer, coons, foxes, skunks, civet cats, regular cats, dogs, quail, pheasants, turkeys, chickens, bears, elephants, lions and tigers. I even *like* mice—in their place. And I don't intend to kill any of them with my pickup. So don't shout at me while I'm driving!"

We rolled on down the road for a few miles in almost complete silence. The sun was gone and except for my headlights, the world was ensconced in darkness. And as we thundered along the road, a myriad of insect life flew in kamikaze formations to end their lives on the windshield of my pickup truck. Soon it was completely covered with their gooey little carcasses.

"Well, it's just too bad you don't *like* bugs." My wife couldn't resist getting the last word in.

WHO'S THE BOSS?

Remember when President Bush was selling his case to invade Iraq? There were plenty of pundits on both sides of the issue. They used all facets of the media: radio, television and newspapers to voice their opinions and push their own agendas. There came a point in time when many Americans were getting weary of all of the war talk. I had a friend tell me that he was tired of the continual debate about whether or not the United States should invade Iraq.

"Let it rest." he said. "Every possible scenario has been visited. Both sides have stated their case, for and against. We don't need to hear anymore about it until we either attack or pull out! Can't you find something else to write about in your column and give us a break?" was his final request.

Well, my friend, news people, including us small-town columnists, are more or less obligated to cover and write about the major events that are going on around the world. It would be nice if the pulse of interest in the nation was beating about something other than an event so cataclysmic as war. We then could pick and choose more mundane subjects to present for public consideration.

But war has always been the *hot topic* and, my duty as a serious columnist requires that I do my best to address all aspects of the *hot topics* that I come across.

So, once again, I have to talk about war, but not the war in Iraq. Nor the possible threat of war with North Korea. Not even the *Cola Wars*. No, we're going to talk about a war that has been raging on for decades right under our very noses. While for the most part, it has been a bloodless conflict, it is a war that has thrown households in America asunder! It has created homes divided against themselves! It has pitted brother against brother, sister against sister and perhaps most devastating, *wife* against *husband*!

I'm talking about the war that takes place in most American households almost every night—the war over the television remote control! For it is understood that he, or she, who controls the televised signals coming into the home, is known throughout the land as the undisputed "Boss of the Household." And I think that we men get a bad rap on this subject, as we are consistently portrayed as unrelenting *control freaks* who carry our remotes all over, even into the bathroom, because we are afraid of losing our control, while most women coyly deny even wanting to control the remote.

But in reality, few are willing to give up the small, wireless, electrical device that is symbolic of being in charge.

While it is an unheralded competition at our house, my wife and I do not see eye-to-eye when it comes to our television viewing and there is an underlying animosity over who controls the remote. If I grab up the remote first, my wife stalks off to bed in disgust. If *she* happens to be the first to take custody of the multi-buttoned channel-changer, she follows a surfing pattern that drives me nuts. If an exciting movie with a stirring theme, some violence, possible nudity, a historic background including horses and six-guns is on, I want to watch it. But she has the remote and says, "I just want to see *what else* is on."—*Immediate flip*—to a very funny half-hour situation comedy featuring a good-looking female main character and a rather dumpy looking male main character. It would be okay with me to watch this, but she's not interested!

Immediate flip—basketball.

Immediate flip—baseball.

Immediate flip—football.

Immediate flip—the Rock-video station featuring a long-haired goofy-looking asshole with a guitar and a microphone into which he is screaming about how much he loves the woman he's cheating on. He's accompanied by a goofy-looking female asshole (as you can see, I'm not a sexist) with a guitar and a microphone into which she is screaming about how much she loves the man she's cheating on—"Let's just watch this one video and then I'll change it." She says with a giggle. She knows how much I hate that crap. True to her word, after it is over . . . *flip*—a John Wayne movie that I could really get into, but . . .

Immediate flip—a program about people letting other people decorate their houses—

"I just think that is so neat," she coos. "We'll just see what they're going to do with this one room, okay?" After they go through changing the carpet, wallpaper, curtains, bedspread and, oh yeah, the lampshade by the rocking chair . . . *flip*—bowling

Immediate flip—golf

Immediate flip—rodeo

"I just hate sports."

Immediate flip—the Country Western-video station featuring the same long-haired goof with a guitar and a microphone singing about how much he loves the woman he's cheating on accompanied by the same female goof with a guitar and a microphone singing about how much she loves the man she's cheating on, only this time they are both wearing cowboy hats—I'm not sure if it's the cowboy hats or the fact that the song is about *cheatin'* that makes it a country song, but I guess it doesn't matter because, guess who wanted to watch it again.

"Let's just watch this one video (again) and then I'll change it."

. . . *flip.*

MASH rerun (I love MASH). "I hate MASH."

Immediate flip—the station where they sell jewelry and women's clothing twenty-three and a half hours a day—"I just want to see what colors that sweater comes in and then I'll change it, okay?"—(Just how damn many colors are there anyway?)

. . . *flip*—a music awards show just getting started!

"We should watch this, but I have to pee, so maybe I'll just watch it up in bed."

A divine act of God!

She lays the remote down and I grab it quicker than a jack rabbit humping a bunny and change channels to the original movie I wanted to watch, which, I might add, is all but over.

Still, whenever a conversation about the TV remote comes up, it is always stated, irrevocably, that *I* am the one who *hogs control* of the remote and that it's really not that important to her. Uh-huh. Then how come when I go up to bed at night and find her sleeping soundly with the bedroom television still on, and I try to turn it off, by using the remote she has clutched in a *death grip* in her hand, she jerks it away from me, and turns the TV off herself without ever waking up?

Is that showing me who's boss or what?

PLANTING THE SEEDS

Well, it seems that time of year when many of us are hit with the uncontrollable urge to get out there and grub around in the dirt has come again. I think the desire for it must be a throw-back to our childhood when getting down on all fours and crawling around in mother earth's freshly tilled soil was irresistible not to mention one whole hell of a lot easier. As you may have already guessed, I'm talking about gardening.

Gardening has always been a pretty big deal at our house. The wife and I meet at the tilled garden's edge to plot out not only what we are going to plant, but where in the garden and how much of each vegetable, we are going to plant. This is a joint effort that sounds simple enough. But let me tell you. It's not. But it is a perfect example of how well we work together.

To put it bluntly, we don't see eye-to-eye very often and when it comes to the garden it becomes somewhat of a contest as to who gets to plant what. My wife likes to plant a wide variety of vegetables, and flowers.

I like to plant sweet corn.

She likes to put in a couple rows of broccoli, some Brussels sprouts, a few hills of summer squash, radishes, carrots, onions and a few rows of green beans.

I like to plant sweet corn.

She is into collard greens, spinach, and leaf lettuce.

I'm into sweet corn.

She likes sweet peas, pod peas and snow peas.

I like sweet corn.

She enjoys the color and variety that homegrown vegetables add to our summer time meals.

I enjoy wallowing elbow deep into a plate of roasted ears flanked by a tub of butter and a salt shaker with large, I said LARGE holes in it.

As you can probably guess, we usually have a few problems when it comes to planning the garden. My wife wields her accustomed weapon, the hoe, leaving me the clumsy rake. She digs the rows because even when

I stake out a string line to follow, my rows "aren't straight." Then it is my job to plant the seed in the rows and cover them up. The seemingly simple process sounds something like this:

"Let's put the radishes along this side, Okay?" she says. (*Translation: We are going to plant the radishes right here, so don't argue.*)

"Okay, but where are we going to plant the sweet corn?" I asked.

"Don't worry about that. We'll get it later." (*Translation: I said don't argue.*)

Right next to the two rows of radishes, she hoes three rows out to put peas in.

"Okay, now let's put the peas in these three rows." (*Translation: Plant the peas and I don't want to hear any lip.*)

"Well, all right, but where was it you're planning to put the sweet corn?" That is me asking again.

"Don't worry about that. We'll get it later." (*Translation: I said, don't give me any lip.*)

Beside the peas comes a couple rows of green beans.

"I think the green beans will do good right here next to the peas, huh?" (*Translation: This is non-negotiable, so just drop the green beans in these rows and stop sniveling.*)

"But, but, what about the sweet corn?" I asked, eyeing the ever shrinking tilled up surface of the back yard.

"Don't worry about that. We'll get it later." (*Translation: I said it wasn't negotiable and I meant it.*)

Carrots are next.

"We'll put these carrots here. They'll look nice growing next to the beans." (*Translation: We're planting these carrots whether you like it or not.*) You ever plant carrots? We always end up with a real nice bunch of carrot tops, but not much for carrots.

"You're not forgetting the sweet corn are you?"

"Don't worry about that. I said we'd get it later." (*Translation: Sheesh.*)

Four hills of cucumbers were next.

"I think if we plant the cucumbers here in this open space, they should have plenty of room to spread out, without crawling all over the rest of the stuff, don't you?" (*Translation: The cucumber is King. We're going to give it its space. End of discussion.*)

"I wonder if we couldn't just plant the corn here with the cucumbers. That way, the cukes can climb around on the corn plants and there will be plenty of room for both." That was me again.

"Don't worry about that. We'll take care of it later." (*Translation: You think you're going to shade MY cucumbers with your stupid corn, HA!*)

Next there were green peppers, red peppers and yellow peppers—very colorful.

"You know, we're just going to have to put all of these peppers right here together." (*Translation: The peppers are going in here and now. And I don't want to hear any whining about it.*)

"You know, we're dang near out of space and we haven't planted a single kernel of corn yet."

"Don't worry about that. We'll take care of it later." (*Translation: I said stop your whining!*)

We planted tomato plants next: 21 red, 4 yellow.

"Now if we spread these tomatoes out just a little more this year, it won't be so hard to get in to pick them this fall." (*Translation: Ha ha, there's no more room for his stupid sweet corn.*)

"But this doesn't leave any room for my stupid sweet corn." I commented as I covered the last tomato plant's roots.

"Really," she says with an evil smile. "Golly, I guess we just forgot all about the sweet corn. Why didn't you say something *before* we planted all of this other stuff?" (*Translation: I wonder if this will work again next year? How stupid is he?*)

IN SEARCH OF NIRVANA

The wife and I took a little vacation last week. I say little, because it only lasted a couple of days. We left Thursday at about 3:05 p.m. and were on our way to Minneapolis, Minnesota. In what has become an unpopular family tradition, when we were about four miles from home, the wife remembered that she forgot to unplug the curling iron in the bathroom before we left. The conversation about this seemingly yearly event went something like this. (I have removed all of the cussing, so it's okay for the kids to read this.)

"I think I forgot to unplug the curling iron."

"So."

"So we just have to go back!"

"Why?"

"Do you want to come home to a burned down house?"

"Are you sure you forgot to unplug *your* curling iron or do you just *think* you forgot to unplug it?"

"What difference does it make? Do you want to worry about the house burning down the whole time we are gone?"

"Okay, Okay! We'll go back."

Argument over. (I'll let you figure out who said what.)

So we turned around and came home. Then the neighbor stopped by and said he had followed us to town and didn't think our brake lights were working. (That's all I need. Imagine driving around the city without brake lights. From past year's driving experience there, I think most Minnesota drivers in the greater Twin Cities metropolitan area are out to kill me anyway. Not having brake lights might just give them the excuse they've been looking for.)

This thought caused a quick trip to the local mechanic for a look-see at the brake lights. But they seemed to be working fine. (Isn't that the way it goes? Take something that isn't working to someone who knows how to fix it and the damn thing starts working without being fixed. (One of God's little jokes!)

We left *again* at 3:45 p.m. with high hopes and a certain knowledge that our motel room would be waiting, no matter how late we arrived. They had my credit card number *and* I called to tell them we'd be late. (I did that before we left the first time . . . we've been on a trip or two before.) This time, the wife didn't remember she had forgotten her cash until we were 72 miles north. (Maybe you shouldn't let the kids read this part.)

"What? We're going on a shopping vacation and you forgot to bring your goddamn money?"

"It's all right. I'll get along without it."

"Wait a damn minute. Are you *sure* you don't want to go back and get *your* money, Honey?"

"No, that's okay. You've got some don't you?"

"Well, yeeeaaah, but we can go back and get yours if you want. Really we can."

"No no, that's all right, we've got your checkbook. I'll get by."

"But we can—"

"I said it's OKAY!"

Argument over. (Go ahead and figure out who said what.)

I'm not sure how long of a trip the wife thought this was going to be because she had packed sandwiches, chips, pretzels, licorice, gummy bears, juice and pop. So I should have known better, but around supper time, when we were near Mankato, I asked the wife if she wanted to eat a sandwich, or go to the Red Lobster.

(Dumb, dumb, dumb!)

I got lost driving around Mankato trying to find the Red Lobster. So finally, after an exorbitant amount of cussing, we settled for an Applebee's. You should already know this, but I'll tell you anyhow. As soon as we were finished eating at Applebee's, we walked out in the parking lot and I looked to my left and saw the Red Lobster sign down the street about a hundred yards and I made the mistake of pointing it out to the wife . . . if looks could kill, I'd be dead. (The wife really likes the Red Lobster.)

We made it to the motel in Burnsville about 9:00 p.m., in plenty of time to get rested up for the Friday morning trip to THE MALL OF AMERICA—the sacrosanct Mecca of shopping. For years I avoided the place by telling the wife I couldn't find it. Which was true. But then she came up with this bright idea of *asking directions* blowing my excuse for staying away right out of the water.

Now I've driven there enough times that I don't have a problem finding it. The problem I do have is when I get there. I know most people will get a chuckle out of this, but my problem is that even though there is about 640 acres of parking around the Mall, I can't seem to find a parking space. It's not because it's full. We're there *before* the joint opens (with bells on - I might add) but there are certain areas closed off, certain areas for valet parking, and numerous one-way and wrong-way signs and I seem to find each and every last one of them by going the *wrong way* on the *one-way* streets!

Sadly it's not only at the MOA (Mall of America) I have this problem. It's every place I go; restaurants, discount stores, malls, and sports arenas. I have a problem following those arrows painted on the lot and end up going down the up aisle and can't park because I'm going the wrong way. Or, I can't find the stupid entrance to even get in the place. Whoever designs these places is just on a completely different plane of existence than I. I always want to turn in near where the front door of the establishment is. But invariably, that is the exit. I also always think the exit should be somewhere at the back of the lot. But of course, that's usually the entrance. Somebody is backwards, and I don't think it's me!

But we finally got parked at the MOA and walked in through the Sears store. As we entered the Mall proper, a great change overtook my wife. She was smiling and happy, and had seemed to forget all of my cussing and our arguing as to who was stupid, me or the guy who designed the parking lot. You could see she had reached an ideal condition and was about to begin experiencing harmony, stability and joy that had put her mind at ease.

But for me, it took a little longer. I was still feeling the tension of the parking lot. It wasn't until I took the escalators to level three of the MOA that I began to experience nirvana. That's where all the food joints are!

ON THE ROAD AGAIN

We took a little trip last week and I thought I'd tell you about some of the events that occurred while we were on the road. Since I don't believe any of you really give a big rat's ass about the lay of the land and the type of farms we saw on the trip, I'm going to skip all of that this time and merely say that if you want to know about the farms and what they looked like in northeastern Iowa, go look for yourself. It's a nice trip and you'll be glad you did.

I am going to say that we stayed one night in Decorah, Iowa at a Country Inn & Suites motel on Iowa Hi-way 9. We were very pleased with our room which featured a king-sized bed, good television, and large spacious bathroom. The staff was very helpful and polite. In fact, the only complaint I might have about the place is that the water in the Jacuzzi was a bit too hot and I woke up in the night and thought my wife had left me.

I'm used to our bed at home, which is of the size that, if I lie on my back and flop my arm out, I can expect to get it flopped (and none too gently) right back in my face, with some sort of complaint about me hitting her in the back of the head. And if she decides to change positions, like from her back to her side or from her side to her stomach, it starts a motion that usually wakens me to the fact that my bladder is in need of relief.

Well she didn't wake me up that night in the motel and when I woke up to answer the "*Call of the Wild Porcelain Bowl*", I had to turn a light on, just to see if she was still in the room. I'm not sure if I never noticed her moving around because the bed was so big or because she wasn't moving. She claims the only reason she changes positions at home is because she's dodging my hand being flopped in her face or the fact that I'm kicking her with my foot when I flop from one side to the other. But I don't believe that, because I usually settle in for the night and I don't notice myself flopping around all that much.

The only real mistake I made that bears much interest to you readers is that I forgot to pack my pants for the trip. I had a couple of pairs of shorts that I could have worn, but my wife got wind of a Wal-Mart in Decorah

117

(That's right, she can smell those places like the rest of us can smell Christmas dinner cooking.) and demanded that I go buy a pair of jeans, *"just in case you need them."* So we spent some "quality time" shopping and she made a big deal out of the fact that I found more to buy than she did. I don't go looking around in a place if I don't intend to buy something. There's the difference between me and my wife. I don't go shopping unless I need something and then if I find what I need, I buy it without a lot of soul searching about whether it's the right color or if it will fit or not. Besides, she's the one who talked me into the shirt and hat to go with my jeans. All I needed was the pants, a bag of popcorn, a bottle of pop, some broad heads for my hunting arrows and that Minnesota Vikings freezer mug.

The only real problem that my little shopping spree at Wal-Mart (buying stuff for myself) caused was that she felt justified in coercing me into spending a certain amount of time in some of the different antique shops that have sprouted from every rock formation, hardware store, restaurant and old school building along the upper Mississippi River in northeast Iowa.

The wife dragged me through a bunch of them in Marquette, Iowa. She showed me how to spend what she called, *quality time* and not spend much money doing it. In other words, it took us what I would call *all day* (she called it a few minutes--we both exaggerate) looking for something for her to buy and when she found a brass hour glass for $10.95 plus tax, it hardly seemed worth the effort it took to find it, to me.

So, as soon as I could pry her out of the antique stores, I gave her a quick lesson on how to spend $20 in ten minutes and have absolutely nothing to show for it. All you have to do is walk onto a riverboat casino, sit down at a blackjack table and lose four hands in a row. Nothin' to it! It was clean. It was quick. It was easy, slam-bam and we were out of there and moving on down the road.

But that's how I am when I'm traveling. I like to keep moving. I don't like getting bogged down in this store or that store. I don't have to worry about whether my hour glass takes an actual hour for the sand to fall from one half to the other or if it might only take nineteen minutes. And I don't have to worry about whether the egg beater I bought later actually had a red handle or if someone painted it red and sanded it off to make it look old and worn.

My money is gone. In one fell swoop, four deals, one shuffle, it's gone and I know where it went. I don't have to worry about whether or not I was gypped. I know I was! I figured I would be when I sat down. I don't have to worry about where I'll set my hour glass or how I'll display my egg beater. I put my money down, came close to winning one hand, got the crap kicked out of me on the other three hands and got a very respectful, *"sorry about that sir,"* as the dealer took my money, and *"better luck next time,"* as I got up to leave the table.

Now that's what I call an expeditious expenditure of time and money!

THE HIGH PRICE OF MILK

I went in to buy a gallon of milk the other day. It cost me $25. *No way,* you say! Not possible. Milk is not that high-priced. Well, just take a gander at my checkbook stub and you will see that I wrote a check to the grocery store for $25 on that day. And all I went in there for was a gallon of milk.

Granted, I came out of there carrying more than just a gallon of milk. I had some ice cream, chocolate topping, a can of pork & beans, a can of peas, a pound and a half of hamburger, a couple of twelve packs of pop, two bags of Corn Nuts, a Snickers bar, and one of those suckers that taste like a caramel apple.

Impulse Buying—that's what it's called. Buying more than what you originally planned to on the mere whim of seeing it. It is a curse that afflicts millions of us Americans each and every day. The thing that bugs me about it is that I was so engrossed in picking out all of that other stuff that *I almost forgot to buy the damn milk*!

If it can be said that we *Impulse Buyers* help out the grocery stores, it has to be stated that we are a regular gold mine for the discount stores. And they are set up to take every advantage of the impulse buyer.

The other day I decided to stop at a discount store and get a quart of oil for my pickup. The place was a mad house. There were people everywhere. But I wasn't going to let that hinder me. I knew what I wanted. I knew where it was. I knew about what it should cost and had enough cash in hand to pay for it. I **was** focused. That is just the way I shop!

I dodged left, then right, avoiding groups of people stalled in the aisle ways. I spun passed a couple of little kids fighting over some toy that they had lifted from the toy department, detoured around a knot of teenagers loitering in the CD and tape area and hit the automotive section without breaking stride. I scooped up a 1 quart plastic jug of the slippery stuff and headed unheeded toward the checkout area.

This is where the story takes a sad turn. Each and every check-out station had at least eight people in it waiting to be checked out. So I made one quick pass, trying to gage by their purchases, which line would move the fastest. I took my place at the end of the line at the middle cash register because most of the people ahead of me appeared to have only one item they intended to purchase. The line should have moved swiftly.

But soon it was apparent that for some reason the line wasn't moving at even a snail's pace. On closer inspection, I noticed that the lady up front had added half a cart full of stuff to the single item she had when I got in line behind her. Consequently, it was taking a while for her to check out. Looking around, I noticed some of the other people in line were reading magazines. One guy was looking over the rack of candy bars.

Finally, that first lady got finished and we moved up one. I did a quick survey of the checkout line in front of me. The second lady only had about four or five items. I noticed the guy two places ahead of me looking through the tobacco products display. The lady right in front of me picked up a bottle of pop. A guy who got in line behind me helped himself to a package of batteries.

The next person whose turn it was to check out only had one item!

Halla—luya!

All he had was a jacket . . . WITH NO PRICE TAG ON IT!

Suddenly, the already crawling pace ground unceremoniously to a complete halt, while they sent someone to find out how much the freakin' jacket cost. The girl they sent must have got lost because she never came back. I wouldn't be surprised to see her picture on a milk carton soon.

So with that line stalled and all of the other lines moving slowly, but steadily, I did the only sane thing to do . . . I jumped over into the next line, giving up two places but at least gaining a line that *was* moving. But the Impulse Buying bug had infected this line too. The man three places ahead of me, picked up a six pack of small Coke bottles. A lady nearer the check out picked up a hand-held calculator. But we *were* moving slowly, but surely, toward *nirvana* in the form of a cash register. Unfortunately, when the lady directly in front of me got to the checkout, it was discovered that she also had one of those jackets with no price tag on it!

"We'll send someone to check that price right away."

Ah, a rack of those little books including the ever-present, calorie counter. Oh, what's this? Cigarette lighters! Here we go, an assortment of different playing cards.

The guy looking for the jacket price *never came back* either! I was beginning to suspect foul play. If they don't have a price on the jackets, they should be free! That's my opinion. But nobody cared what I thought.

So I jumped three lanes over to the left after making sure none of the people in front of me was carrying a jacket. After only a few short delays, for people to get their impulse buying in, I moved uninhibited up to the checkout register. Just when I was about to step up and take my turn, the checkout lady said,

"BREAK TIME"

Son of a bitch!

I was about to come unglued! But before I popped a main vein, a sweet young thing stepped in to take her place at the checkout. Her quick action not only saved me from having a stroke, she also probably kept me from going to jail.

She began checking me out, which if I had just had my quart of oil to pay for wouldn't have taken long. But because of all of the time I had spent standing in three different lines, waiting, my impulses had kind of taken over. I had: microwave popcorn, two candy bars, some size C batteries, the *National Enquirer*, a calorie counter, a can of peanuts, a bottle of cold pop, a six-pack of warm pop, some breath mints, Rolaids, a bag of chips, a York Peppermint Pattie, a car-buying manual, two Slim Jims, one beef jerky, a calculator, and a pack of cigarettes. (I don't even smoke, and never have. But waiting in the checkout line was about enough to make a guy want to start.) Oh, and my quart of oil.

Needless to say, I had to write a check.

DEPARTMENT STORE DREAMIN'

"There are only 76 more days 'til Christmas!" And who knows how many of them will be designated as "SHOPPING DAYS?" Doesn't that just curdle the cockles of your heart?

What brought this on, you ask? Well, the other day, I got hornswoggled into going into a department store with my wife. Hornswoggled may be a strong term, but I thought this was to be a quick, in and out, type of shopping trip and I truly believe it would have been if it had not been for the fact that there, cluttering up the shelves were all kinds of Christmas decorations!

For cryin' out loud. Halloween isn't even here yet. These stores haven't even had a good chance at pushing a bunch of candy down our throats for that holiday yet and they're already trying to ruin what used to be my favorite holiday. Needless to say, my wife shares no such feelings on this matter. She was tickled pink that the Christmas decorations were on display.

I was adamant. I absolutely refused to walk through that area and look at that stuff. Trouble is, my wife was adamant too. So we had to compromise. I walked through, *but I didn't look at anything.* But of course, my wife looked at enough for both of us. In fact it wasn't long before she got so carried away that I had no problem slipping away to the TV section where I tuned in a ball game and was reasonably happy until all of a sudden I heard some official sounding guy on the store's intercom system saying "Attention Shoppers. It's now 8:45 and in 15 minutes, we will be closing. Please bring your purchases to the checkout, NOW."

I jumped up and beat a hasty retreat out of there.

Getting locked in a Department store overnight has always been one of my greatest nightmares. My wife however, has no such fears and was nowhere to be seen. I quickly looked around for her, thinking that maybe she had actually vacated the premises before me. That thought left my mind when I heard the next announcement.

"The store will be closing in five minutes. Thank you for shopping with us, but yes, you have to leave!" the intercom guy stated rather sternly.

There was a slow trickle of last minute shoppers coming through the checkout line and I noticed that some of the lights in the back part of the building were going out. But there was still no sign of the mother of my children.

Since she started working a steady job, it has really put a slow down on how often she gets to go shopping and has even put a severe crimp on her yearly CRAZY DAYS outings and her GARAGE SALE attendance has fallen way off too. So you really can't blame her for taking advantage of the opportunity to shop when it comes along. After all, shopping is her favorite sport and I wouldn't like it if I had to give up watching football.

But what she doesn't seem to understand is that, to the people who work in Department Stores, they are not like the place you want to go when you die, they are merely a place they have to be to make a living and when closing time comes, they want to go home.

"All right lady, we're lockin' up and you're leaving" came the voice over the loud speaker, and then, "GET 'ER, BOYS!"

There was a loud rustling back in the car care section as a herd of sales people converged on the lone hapless woman whom they dragged, kicking and screaming to the front of the store and delivered into my custody. One softhearted sales person stated gently, "You can come back tomorrow."

Well, before everybody calls my wife and asks her if this is true, I may as well fess up. We did go to the store. She did drag me through the CHRISTMAS STUFF and when the guy locked the door behind her when we left, he did invite her to come back the next day.

The rest is my imagination and yes, my imagination does get me in trouble occasionally.

MURDER IN THE CHECKOUT LINE

Probably the thing that bugs me most about shopping is when I go into a store, pick out what I want to buy, and then have to go stand in the checkout line for twice as long as it took me to find the item. I would like to be able to checkout in less time than it will take my infant grandson to graduate from high school! But an experience I had at a local department store the other night, made getting out of there before he graduates from college seem "iffy."

I needed some new razors. So I stopped in and grabbed a package of throw-aways while the wife picked up a few things she needed. When we were ready to go, I surveyed the checkouts looking for the shortest line and ducked into the one with only one lady in front of me. The wife went into the line beside it where there were about six other shoppers standing. *Warning: The shortest line isn't always the quickest.* (Somehow, my wife knows this.)

The woman in front of me only had a half cart full of stuff to check out. I thought I would be checked out in plenty of time to start whining at the wife to hurry up. (That bugs the hell out of her.) My checkout girl didn't show any tendencies toward being a rocket scientist. It might have helped if she was. Even so, I couldn't really blame what happened next on her. She slid the first item across the scanner . . . and the lady said, "I have a coupon for that" and handed the coupon to the checker. She slid the next item across . . . and the lady said, "I have a coupon for that" and handed another coupon to the checker. She slid the third item across the scanner, and the lady said . . . "I have a coupon for that too."

"Just hold on to your coupons until I get everything scanned." The checker girl, starting to get confused, told her adding, "Then I'll subtract all of the coupons at once." By this time I'm getting a little antsy. The checkout girl in the wife's line was scanning people right on through without a single *coupon*, or *price check* to slow her down and the wife had already moved up into a tie with me as *the next to be checked out*. I could see she had that certain look of *smugness* that professional athletes get in their eyes when they are at the top of their game and they know everybody knows it.

But by now, the rocket scientist was happily scanning away—fourth—fifth—sixth item scanned and already in the computer/cash register—seventh—eighth—ninth . . .

"Uh oh," she said, eyeballing item number six as she shoved it in a bag to make room on the counter, "I'm gonna have to see your ID."

What's this? This lady wasn't buying any booze. They don't even sell it in that department store! I hadn't seen any tobacco products go across the scanner (and I was watching.)

"Yes," the rocket scientist said as she unscanned all of the items she had just scanned until she got back to the infamous item #6. "I got in trouble the other day for not checking a person's ID to make sure they were 21 before I sold them a bottle of these."

"What? What is she talking about?" my mind was screaming as I saw the wife open her purse to pay for what she had bought.

The item of her concern was nothing more than a bottle with what looked to be orange jawbreakers in it. The lady in front of me giggled nervously and said, "I've never been carded before." I had to wonder why, she didn't look a day over *FIFTY-THREE!*

"These are for my 20 year old son, I'm certainly not going to use them." she added defensively. (By this time, my wife was checked out and sitting on a bench near the door . . . *smiling smugly while waiting for me.*)

I couldn't figure out what all the hubbub over a few orange jawbreakers was all about. My wife, the professional shopper, informed me later that the orange "jawbreakers" were actually paintballs that some people use as ammunition when they play cowboys and Indians. So they have to make sure no little kids under the age of 21 get their hands on them.

Oh.

But the rocket scientist had to go check with her supervisor to see if she could sell them to the lady, even though the lady had admitted that she was buying them for her underage son.

So what we had here was a rocket scientist determined to card a woman clearly past the age of pink hair and pierced eyebrows, because she got in trouble for not carding someone who probably *was* underage the other day, *AND* a coupon collector, who was clearly old enough to know better, admitting that she was buying them for someone who couldn't legally buy them himself.

The girl came back and handed the lady her ID and scanned the paint balls, (a sale is a sale, I guess) and the rest of her items, as if none of this had ever come up. By the time all of her items had been checked, I had stood in the line so long that I was fairly sure I'd missed the presidential election.

When the checkout girl finally told the woman that the total came to $63.37, the lady pulled out a mitt full of coupons and wagged them at the checker, saying "don't forget my coupons."

The checker started going back through the already bagged items, item by item, trying to match the items purchased with the coupons handed in. And to top that off, she had to discuss each and every one of them with the coupon lady.

"Boy, you sure have a lot of coupons."

"Well, you can save a lot of money with coupons."

"Oh yeah! This one is worth a quarter, that one, a dime—now did you buy two packages of batteries? I'll have to go ask my supervisor if I can give you coupon credit on both battery coupons—that would be fifty cents off you know."

I swear, the guy behind me, who had been in line about half as long as me, was starting to grow a beard *right before my very eyes.*

"Did you have a beard when you first got in this line?" he asked with a confused, but friendly smile.

That was it for me! I set the razors down and walked out. If I had stood around for even another 5 minutes, waiting to see if the coupon lady could save three whole bucks on a $60 purchase, I just may have grabbed up a paintball gun and used some of her ammo!

MANNEQUINS

I thought I was going nuts the other day. What would make a guy like me think that I was going off the deep end? It all started when I took my wife to Sioux City shopping last Saturday. Considering how well I like to shop, the fact that I took her there in the first place might be a good argument for placing me under supervised care. But I've worked very hard on my anti-shopping attitude and after a few minor adjustments have made some great progress.

The way it used to be was enough to drive a person of my personal shopping persuasion, completely and totally up a tree! A shopping trip with my wife used to be pure torture. I followed her around, whining like a small child. I was bored. I was tired. I was ready to go home. And that was after only the first five minutes in the first store.

In my defense, I would have to say that it is no wonder that I would be bored, tired and ready to go home, when following my wife around shopping. She's a boring shopper. That's right. All she wants to look at is clothes, jewelry, trinkets to set around the house and non-ingestible products that come in bottles or cans. (She calls them hair care products.) "Wouldn't this border look pretty in the dining room? Isn't that the most beautiful color of finger nail polish you've ever seen? Which shirt do you like, the peach or the pale blue? Smell this . . . now this. Which scent do *you* like the best?"

I have had sex with this woman. She knows that I'm not female, yet she was bound and determined to use me as a gal pal when we went to the mall. But I would never play along.

My answers to her questions were: "I didn't know we were gonna re-paper the dining room. I don't like any color of finger nail polish. The blue one. (So she bought the peach.) It's hard to decide which scent I like the best - neither of them smell much like pepperoni."

She's not interested in anything that I am. As far as I'm concerned, if you can't watch it, read it, play with it, or eat it, why would you want it. I'm big on looking at the DVD section, the book section, the sporting goods section and the lunch counter, snack bar or grocery section of any store in the shopping mall. In fact, if there are no food stuffs included in a store's inventory, I'd just as soon not go in to it.

Finally one day I told her that I would quit following her around whining, if she would just quit looking at boring stuff. And she told me that she'd quit looking at boring stuff, if I'd just quit following her around whining. It was kind of a "catch 22" type of a situation. Needless to say, the above mentioned shopping habits, both mine and my wife's, have led to some pretty unhappy shopping trips in the past. But like I said, I've been working on my attitude, and so has my wife (been working on my attitude).

But I think that we've finally come up with a solution to the problems we've experienced while shopping in the past. We set a time and place to meet and then she goes her way and I go mine. Her way is still to walk around all of the stores looking at every boring thing you can think of. My way is to high-tail it to the nearest movie theater, buy a ticket, stop at the snack bar, buy the bushel basket sized bag of popcorn and the fifty-five gallon drum sized soft drink and sit on my butt for two hours while she's out walking her little footsies down to the nubbins!

It works well. When it's time for us to meet, she's usually leg weary, but happy and I'm usually stuffed to the gills and have to pee like a race horse, but happy. So we go home in a good mood instead of being half mad at each other.

When we first get to the mall, I usually run down to the theater to see what is showing and when. Based on that information we decide what time and where to meet after the movie is over. So last Saturday we arrived at the mall and I left her at a jewelry counter (which will keep her transfixed like a moth around a light bulb) and ran down to check out what was showing. On my way to the theater, while passing one of those boring clothing stores, I happened to glance at the mannequins in the window. (This is where things start getting strange.) I swear to God, one of those mannequins winked at me! But I was in a hurry so I didn't pause. I checked out the movies, made my decision and was hurrying back to tell the wife what was what. When I passed that same clothing store window, I was sure the other mannequin (which looked exactly like the first mannequin) blinked both of her eyes.

Like I said, I was in a hurry to catch my wife before the lure of the shiny lights in the jewelry store wore off, so I didn't stop. I admit though, that I was beginning to think something was wrong with either my eyesight or my mind. I told the wife, I'd meet her in 2½ hours and hustled back toward the theater. This time as I passed that window, the mannequins were *sitting down* and I'm not kidding you . . . they *both* smiled at me.

I damn near twisted an ankle coming to a stop! I thought I must have been losing my mind, but I wasn't going to let a little thing like insanity make me late for the movie. After the movie was over though, I went and got my wife, because she knows about these sorts of things and took her back to the store with the winking, smiling mannequins.

With her experienced eye, it didn't take long for her to point out to me that they were actually living *twin sisters* who were only working as mannequins. What a relief! I wasn't going nuts. I took off, heading into the clothing store.

"Where are you going?" the wife asked. "I thought you were in a hurry to go home."

"Looking for the flimsy lingerie section." I answered. "We got plenty of time."

PART THREE

THE RELUCTANT SHOPPER

Well, I wasn't as smart as I thought I was going to be last Friday, the day after Thanksgiving.

The business world loves *Black Friday*, because it is the busiest shopping day of the year! I hate *Black Friday* because, *it's the busiest friggin' shopping day of the year!*

I intended to go hunting with a friend and let the wife go shopping all by herself. But then my friend said he couldn't go hunting. (I figure the poor bastard probably had to go shopping with his wife.)

Unfortunately, as I indicated earlier in this memoir, my wife's goal in life is to drag me along shopping with her on the Day After Thanksgiving. She'll never admit it. She always claims that it is worse taking me shopping than it was taking the kids when they were little. The only difference is that I don't need her to help me when I have to go to the bathroom. However, she never likes it when I get lost and have the store page her, because I can't find her and am pretty sure she has abandoned me and went home.

So, she will tell you that she *doesn't even want me to go along*. She claims to have grown tired of my whining and crying about being tired and bored and wanting to go home, years ago. Yet she still finds ways to either coerce me into accompanying her, or she out and out, bribes me. In other words, if she can't find somebody else to go with her, I'm better than nothing.

Things weren't so bad when the department stores had their televisions hooked up to cable and I could tune in a ball game or an old movie to spend my day of shopping watching TV. But now, they've opted to hook them all to a VCR and they show little kids' movies on all of the sets in the building. (That wouldn't be so bad, but I've seen them all at least a dozen times!)

After my friend backed out on me last Friday, she casually mentioned that since I wasn't going hunting she could *sure* use some "help" Christmas shopping. But let's face it, I'm pretty worthless when it comes to helping with the Christmas shopping. Just look at all the times I have walked into a store, walked right up to an object, picked it up and said that I thought it would be a good gift for this person or that person, only to have her tell me that it wouldn't be at all appropriate.

She has this idea that you need to worry about whether the people you buy something for will like it or not. And in order to find a suitable gift, you have to look at everything in the store, before making your selection. I live under the belief that if I buy something and give it to someone, they are going to like it, because **I** gave it to them. If not, that's their problem, not mine. I fulfilled my obligation. I gave them a gift. They can do with it as they please; like it, lump it, or throw it in the corner and forget it. So Christmas shopping trips with my wife usually end up with a conflict of opinions and I generally try to avoid going with her.

I told her that I was thinking of raking leaves. She knew that was a lie. I haven't raked a leaf in over twenty years and don't intend to for twenty more. You see, I'm a charter member of LRA (Leaf Rakers Anonymous) and can't stand to get anywhere near a rake or I might lose control. You see, I can't be trusted to not burn the rake, right along with the pile of leaves.

So then I told her I was thinking about mowing the lawn *one last time* for the year. She knew that was a bald face lie too. You see, I have this little rule-to-live-by that I've lived by for my entire adult life. I don't mow the lawn after October 1st.

So then I mumbled something about *maybe, thinking about, possibly, considering,* working on cleaning up the basement . . . maybe. That didn't fly either. She ignored that attempt to put her off, stating that she wanted for us to *get up early, get there early,* and *get back early*. But I was quick to identify that that was just a play on my famous old saying, *"Let's get going, so we can get back."*

Then I took some of the mumble out of my voice and tried to sound a little more sincere about *maybe, possibly, thinking about, considering* starting on remodeling the bathroom by *starting to, get ready to, prepare to, round up everything* I need to, get started installing the ceiling tile.

There must have been a little too much procrastination in my tone of voice or something, because I really thought that would be something she would go for. She's been after me to do that for months. But I guess that she must have wondered if maybe it might take me all morning to get ready to do the job and then I would run out of time before I had to leave on my hunting trip. (In a totally unrelated topic, do you think there is anything to this *mind reading* you hear so much about?)

She finally got tired of this line of conversation and offered to buy me breakfast if I went with her, so I went.

What can I say? I'm just an old Egg McMuffin whore.

TRAIL MIX

Picture this scenario: We're in a grocery store and the wife is looking for a certain mix of items to make a recipe she picked up while watching QVC. That is one channel that came with cable TV which allows my wife to do her favorite past time (shopping) while sitting at home if she wants to. She heard them talking about this great "trail-mix" recipe on QVC and wanted to buy the stuff so she could make it for us to eat at home. (You don't have to actually be on the trail to eat trail-mix you know.)

I'm a bit skeptical about a lot of the "trail-mixes" that are offered around. They usually contain foods that are high in sugar designed to give you energy, something salty to keep you sweating, and high fiber foods to, well . . . keep you regular I guess. That is where I have my problem. Some of that fibrous stuff isn't fit for birds to gnaw on. It's grainy, hard to chew and scratches you, both on the way in and again on the way out a few hours later. Another main-stay of many "trail-mixes," it seems, is raisins. I hate raisins. There is nothing like putrid grapes to ruin a good cookie, a nice pan of bars, or "trail mix" for that matter. That's what they are you know, grapes that have gone bad.

Since the recipe my wife was considering consisted of only three ingredients including salted peanuts, M&M's and candy corn (no putrid grapes) I was all for it. In the M&M's you've got your sugar, and in the candy corn, you've got your sugar and in the peanuts, you've got a little salt (I like salt) and carbohydrates which (you might have guessed) will turn into sugar!

I *was* in a hurry as usual, so I thought I'd help things along a little by picking up the ingredients while she shopped. I grabbed a can of peanuts and a bag of M&M's and was scouring the candy section for candy corn when she caught up with me.

The only thing that dragged her away from her shopping was the fact that she knew I'd get the wrong stuff for her trail mix. How did she know? Because I always pick out the wrong stuff. Whether it's picking the ingredients for trail-mix or buying a bucket of swamp scum. I assure you, I wouldn't be able to get swamp scum that was up to her standards for swamp scum. It would be too green or too brown or too thick or too runny or it would have too much slime on the top or not enough slime on top. She's pretty much a perfectionist in all things and if she were to buy a bucket of swamp scum you can bet it would have to meet up to her standards or she wouldn't buy it. And if she did buy it, you can bet your ass it would be the best swamp scum money could buy. (She has very expensive tastes.)

Which brings us back to the trail-mix stuff. She caught up with me in the checkout line just as I was about to check out and began pointing out my mistakes. She wanted the hull-less, lightly salted party peanuts instead of the saltier than the rim of a margarita glass, jumbo redskins that come out of the can dripping in their own oil. (Just the kind I like.) And my choice of M&M's was totally unacceptable, too. They were the regular M&M's. You know, the little round, brown, red, green, yellow and orange plain M&M's. She wanted the "fall"-colored M&M's. I guess the main difference between regular M&M's and "fall"-colored M&M's is that the red, green, yellow and blue ones are left out of the bag leaving just brown and orange.

I was a bit confused by this, but I was quick to tell her that they didn't have any "fall"-colored M&M's. The guy checking us out suggested that she could just pick out the yellow, red, and green ones which just won him a baleful glare from the wife. The store manager was called into the fray and when my wife requested "fall"-colored M&M's. He looked at her like she was wearing her shirt inside-out (as had both the checkout guy and myself when she told us about them) and then told her that they had pastel M&M's at Easter time and green & red M&M's at Christmas time and red, white and blue M&M's on the 4th of July, but there was no such thing as "fall"-colored M&M's.

That was kind of like throwing down a gauntlet in front of the wife! All of you store managers out there, here's a word of advice. If *my* wife comes up to you and asks for something, no matter how crazy or off-the-wall it is and no matter if you've ever heard of it or not, take her word for it. There is *such a thing*. Don't tell her it doesn't exist. I'm telling you now. She knows more about it than you do! If she says there is gray-green swamp scum with just the right amount of slime around the edges, take her word for it and agree. If you don't have it, just tell her you'll try to get it for her. And if she tells you there are "fall"-colored M&M's, believe her, there is.

We left that store without the ingredients for her trail-mix and went to another store where she found not only "fall" (brown and orange) M&M's, but a nice bag of candy corn and the lightly salted peanuts. She wanted to take that bag of "fall"-colored M&M's back to the first store and rub the manager's nose in it, but as I said, I *was* in a hurry, (Besides, I get squeamish at the sight of a store manager squirming around as he tries to explain to my wife why he didn't know something was available.) and we came on home instead.

When we got home, she dumped the peanuts, "fall"-colored M&M's and candy corn in a little pumpkin shaped jar and stirred them all up.

"There," she said, "isn't that pretty."

That's when it dawned on me that this trail-mix was just for looks, not eating.

HOW TO SAVE MONEY

Well, I went on my first big shopping trip since the Christmas season last Sunday. By "big shopping trip," I don't mean that we went far away and stayed for an extended time. We just ran to one of the local area department stores and were only gone from home for a couple of hours. When the wife first suggested going shopping Sunday, I was what you might call *lukewarm* to the idea.

"What . . . Are you crazy? The Super Bowl is on Sunday!"

She kept her cool and responded that she just wanted to go take a quick look at the "baby stuff" (we have another grandchild) and see if the store had received a shipment of one particular brand of "baby stuff" that she has been looking for and hasn't been able to find because it has been all sold out.

"But the Super Bowl is only on once a year and it's the last football game that I will be able to watch FOR A WHOLE YEAR and—"

"Oh quit whining." She cut my whining off, "I assure you that we can make it to the store, look quickly through the "baby stuff" and be back in plenty of time for the kick-off." Then she said the magic words . . . *"I'll buy you a pizza."* and the next thing I knew, my stomach was leading me out the door with my truck keys in hand.

The subject of the conversation while driving to the store started out being about what kind and what size the pizza should be, but somehow got switched to the fact that I have no pants to wear. Well, I shouldn't use the word *no*, I should say, *hardly any*. I don't know what happened, but according to the wife, who washes my clothes, all of my jeans have worn out at the same time.

One of what I called my "good" jeans had a small hole in the crotch, near the zipper and all of a sudden, the small hole became a big hole. I don't know why, but every time I went to sit down, the hole ripped a little bit bigger and in the space of one afternoon, my only pair of "good" jeans had become my "I can't wear them in public or I'll be arrested" jeans. And then two pairs of my "work" jeans developed *key pocket cancer*. That's when the denim material covering the pocket that you put your wad of keys in, starts to turn white, then gets stringy, and suddenly pops into a full blown hole. Don't misunderstand, the pocket itself may be fine. It's just the material that rides about mid-thigh, right where my keys live when they are not in the ignition of my truck that is affected.

It takes a while, but once the white strings that are woven with the blue strings to make denim, start showing, it's only a matter of time until the condition spreads over the entire thigh area. And then suddenly, the fabric is gone and another good pair of "work" jeans has passed over to the other side. This happened to two pairs of my "work" jeans within a week of each other. I nursed them along for as long as I could, but with the temperatures staying down below freezing, having a hole in the upper thigh area of your pants makes it a bit breezy walking to and from the parking lot at work. So I had to retire them the other night.

My way of retiring old clothing is a bit different. You see, I have a tendency to want to keep wearing it even though for common decency's sake, it should be thrown away. But you see, if I throw it away, I *have* to buy new. I don't like to buy new. So when I retire it, I rip whatever the holey clothing happens to be into such a condition that if I wore it, I could be arrested for indecent exposure. That way, *I'm forced to buy new*.

So on the way to the store, it was decided that since I'm down to one pair of "good" jeans and one pair of "work" jeans (that are also starting to show signs of key-pocket cancer), that I should probably buy a couple of pairs of jeans.

I did. They were only $15 each (a far cry from the $50-a-pair jeans my kids and wife *like* to buy) and I was feeling pretty good.

But then the shopper in my life, who was looking for me, while I was in the little cubby-hole they let you try jeans on in, found some incredible bargains. And they were *all* for me.

I'm not kidding. She found me a camouflage hunting shirt and pants (at half price), a new fishing reel that I've been looking at (on sale), 18 Top-Flite golf balls for $11 (I'm always needing golf balls, especially cheap golf balls), an orange insulated hunting cap ($3) and then I found some lead-heads I've been looking for (they weren't on sale, but they're pretty cheap anyway).

As usual, when I checked-out, the lady in front of me had a coupon that would save her 30 cents if she bought a second bottle - but the coupon wasn't good in that store—but it was locally advertised—but that was last week . . .

I changed lanes three times and finally made it out of the store after only having spent $92 and change.

NINETY-TWO DOLLARS!

I was sick to my stomach. I had only planned on spending $20, had compromised up to $30 and then blown more than $90!

All the way home, my wife tried to explain to me that I had actually *saved* money. I contended that I didn't *save* money. I *spent* money. I just don't understand how if you spend $92, you have saved anything. It is beyond my comprehension. I thought saving is when you put money in the bank and don't spend it.

No, my wife explained—you save money when you spend it buying items you need that are on *sale!*

Well, if that is true, we're in a lot better shape than I thought. In fact, I should be able to retire soon because it seems to me that even though our house is just full of stuff we never even use, it's okay because we've saved so much money by buying it on sale.

A GOOD SCOUT

I was parked in a K-Mart parking lot the other night and a pickup truck pulled in right next to mine. The wife had gone in the store already, as I had elected to just sit there in the parking lot and enjoy the solitude rather than get involved with the hustle and bustle of more after-Christmas sale bargain hunting. I had been sitting there for about five minutes, listening to a basketball game, when this truck pulled in next to me. The driver got out and I heard her speaking to her passenger.

"Watch the truck, Blackie. Don't bark at everyone who walks by, don't slobber on the windows and don't you dare pee on the seat." she instructed in a stern voice. Then she slammed the door and walked toward the automatic sliding doors at the entrance of the store.

I glanced over and saw a big black Labrador Retriever who was shyly looking over at me out of the corner of his eye. When he saw me looking at him, he quickly turned to look straight out the windshield, his head tilted back in a noble pose; head back, chest out, eyes straight forward.

God, what a magnificent creature. His appearance was almost regal. Like a sentry on duty, vigilant, proud and loyal.

I've always liked black Labs. Labrador Retrievers come in all sizes and colors any more, but my favorite is still the black ones. I remember, as a kid growing up, Ernie Tigges, the local druggist had a big black Lab. His name was King. And his stature and bearing certainly legitimized his name. He often stood on the flat roof of their front porch (No, he didn't jump up there. They had a door from an upstairs room that opened onto it.), and guarded their house. He was always friendly and nice when I went to collect from the Tigges's for the newspaper I delivered to their home. But if you happened to walk by their house at night, or approach the door when no one was home, he stood on the porch roof with raised hackles and a gruff warning bark to back off. He was a loyal dog doing his job.

My brother-in-law used to have a little black Lab female. Nickademus was her name. We called her Nikki and she loved to hunt pheasants. She was a flusher, not a pointer, and she did retrieve the bird when you knocked one down. She had a special knack, especially when we were hunting in deep snow, of catching the pheasants alive and bringing them back.

She wasn't particularly "soft" mouthed though, and often, when she "retrieved" a bird she caught on her own, it was dead by the time she handed it over. The big problem with that was that she was an equal opportunity bird catcher. She didn't differentiate between roosters and hens and sometimes we'd end up with a dead hen on our hands. But she meant no harm and certainly thought she was just doing her job; loyally and reliably.

I had a black Lab female once. Her name was Ink. She wasn't nearly as good of a pheasant dog as was Nikki. She was a pretty good duck hunting dog though. She loved the water and loved to swim. She'd break ice, swim in a current and slough her way through two feet of muck and mud to do a fetch job.

Old Ink was a good hound. She'd play with kids or adults and treated everybody with respect. Her main fault was that she trusted everybody on two feet and was overly friendly. I almost lost her when someone dumped a bunch of fish heads in her kennel, and Ink, always wanting to appear grateful for an unexpected feeding, chowed down on them. Fish bones are toxic to dogs and it very nearly killed her. But to her, eating those fish heads was just part of doing her job: being loyal, reliable and trusting.

My son has a big black Lab. Coal weighs one hundred and seventeen pounds and he is full of piss and vinegar. Since Coal is sometimes a house dog and is as big as he is and as rambunctious as he can be, my son decided to take him to some obedience classes. And while he still wags his tail like a weapon when happy or excited, he "sits," "lies down," and "stays" on command with the best of them.

I sat looking over at the Lab in the truck beside me and felt a kind of admiration for him. His dark, gentle eyes were filled with something akin to compassion and held a keen solemn intelligence. He knew what his job was and who it was he wanted to please. I couldn't help but draw a comparison and almost felt a kinship with the dog.

When we had pulled into the parking lot, my wife told me to "go up the end parking lane and park in the third spot," which I did. She had other instructions for me too, if I was staying in the truck.

"If you are going to sit out here listening to the game and the Hawkeyes start losing, don't be shouting curses at the radio. Don't let the windows get all fogged up. Don't make a big mess in here with your pop glass and potato chip bag. And if you decide to come in to the store, make sure you lock the doors!"

As I sat looking at the dog, I choked back a curse as my Hawkeyes fell even further behind, turned off the engine and shut down the defrost fan, crumpled up my pop cup and stuffed it and my empty chip bag in my jacket pocket and punched the lock button on the door as I climbed out of my truck to go in the store.

Yep I couldn't help comparing myself with that dog in the truck next to me. We were both trustworthy, loyal, reliable, and *trained well enough to not pee on the seat.*

COLOR BLIND

I have a slight problem with colors. In fact, I lost a $5 bet back when I cleaned carpet for a living, as to whether a carpet I had cleaned was green or brown. I said it was brown, this guy I bet with said it was green. I still say that we were talking about the color of the carpet *before* we cleaned it, not after.

But I paid up and didn't whine. The bad part is that now I have the reputation of being color blind. Not true. I can tell red from blue, and green from yellow, and I hardly ever miss on white from black. I have a friend who claims he's so color blind that he can't tell the difference between the green, yellow and red traffic lights. But I doubt being color blind would get him out of a ticket for running a stop light. So being that color blind would be a big problem.

I have an entirely different problem. The wife tells me that I have trouble differentiating between the different shades of white. (?) My wife, who is an artist, can distinguish the difference between a lot of shades of many different colors, including the umbers and the siennas. She can blend the different colors to make even different colors and has a sharp eye for contrasting tints and is familiar with all the hues of a rainbow.

Now me, I'm a little less perceptive when it comes to recognizing the wide range of colors. I like the sky to be blue, the ground to be green if it is covered with grass or brown if its dirt. I like the clouds to be white or gray, barns to be red and houses to be white. Not off-white. (How many shades of "off-white" can there be, you ask? A hell of a lot more than you'd think, let me tell ya!)

The problem began years and years ago when we decided to cover one wall in our living room by cutting and fitting 12 inch square mirror panels and sticking them on it, leaving only three walls in the living room to paint. A few weeks ago, one of the mirror panels up near the ceiling came loose and fell. Luckily, it was one of the mirrors behind my wife's chair and not mine. I say this because my wife hardly ever reclines her chair. (If she goes out of the vertical position for more than a couple of minutes, she is very apt to fall asleep.) Now I, on the other hand, recline my chair all of the time. (And I hardly ever fall asleep.) The point is, if the mirror would have been one on my side, estimating the distance out from the wall that it landed, in relation to the distance from the wall my head is when I'm at full recline, it would have decapitated me as surely as if I were on the wrong side during the French revolution.

So, to avoid the very real chance of becoming dead meat while watching TV, we removed all of the mirrors. The bad news is that the wall behind those mirrors hasn't been painted for over twenty years. I couldn't see any real problem with that. The wall looked more or less, white to me just like the other three walls. The wife, however, took great umbrage with me and reiterated her belief in my color blindness. She said it looked terrible! You know what that means.

It's Time To Paint The Living Room!

Man, am I ever sorry that mirror fell off! Jeez, am I ever sorry that stuff holding the mirror to the wall gave loose! (And after only twenty-some years, too.) Boy-oh-boy am I ever sorry we didn't just paint that wall in the first place. Maybe if we had, we wouldn't be painting the whole damn room now!

The thing that I don't understand is that even though she's established that I have problems when it comes to identifying different shades of colors, she drug (dragged?) my sorry butt around to all of the stores that sell paint and pitched a tent by the color charts in each and every one of them. When I started whining about not wanting to spend all day picking out a color, she said not to worry because we were just going to paint the room white anyway. Then she began to show me the paint samples I could choose from.

"*Mesquite*, or *Sea Shell* or *Tumble Weed?*" she asked, holding up three white tiles. "Or maybe, *Sherman's Gray?*" I was already going cross-eyed. "Or how about, *Chiffon Lace? Satin Mist?* Or *Angel's Shower?*"

Honest to God, they all looked white to me. There might have been a slight variance in how the colors looked if you held your hand over one of them, putting it in the shade, while leaving the others in bright light. But other than that, I couldn't see a bit of difference between any of them. To me, they would all be called white and I told her so.

"Oh no!" she exclaimed. "Can't you see the difference? They're off-white. They are really nowhere near white!" and she picked up a chart from farther down the rack. The color on it said, *Snow White*, and she held it next to the color charts we had been looking at and she added, "See how different they are?"

No.

But I stood there, very solicitously and tried to take a very real interest. (Actually, I couldn't give a big rat's ass what color she paints the living room, just so long as she doesn't get between me and the TV while she's doing it.) Yet, all of them appeared to be white to me—maybe not *Snow White*, but they certainly weren't red, blue, green, yellow or black, which, if you look at your primary color chart that only leaves *white*.

But rather than make a federal case out of it, I just fell back to looking at the names and deciding which name I liked best. Like, I could handle watching TV in a room the color of *Mesquite* or even *Sea Shell*. There's something almost macho about a room the color of *Tumble Weed*. And I would much rather tell my friends that I picked out a paint color for our living room called, *Sherman's Gray* than tell them "I really really liked *Chiffon Lace*, but absolutely adored the *Satin Mist!*"

So I told her I liked either *Mesquite* or *Sherman's Gray*. Not surprisingly, she didn't get either one of them. Surprisingly though, instead of *Chiffon Lace* or *Satin Mist*, she opted for a color she hadn't even showed me, called *Tortilla*.

Imagine that. I'm watching television in a room that is the same color as a *Soft Shell Taco!* No wonder I get hungry about 10:00 every night!

A LIFE INSURANCE CONDUNDRUM

Let me set up a scenario for you to consider: A man's wife turns the gas on in his barbeque grill. After trying for three or four minutes to light it using the "spark-light" feature that doesn't work (they never work), she closes the grill lid and leaving the gas on, goes into the house to nag her hubby to get up off his "dead-ass" and go out and light the grill.

Well, it just so happens, that he is watching a ball game and has to wait for the inning to end before he is going anywhere, especially out to light the grill! You all know how long it takes for an inning of baseball to pass, especially when you have something else you really need to do.

So finally, when he climbs up out of his Easy-Boy and ambles out to the grill, he is alert enough to notice that the cold-one he is drinking feels a little light and has developed little sweat bubbles on the side of the can, but fails to realize that the gas knob on the grill was left on the "Light" setting. He also fails to notice the strong odor of gas and is blissfully ignorant that a pretty good amount of flammable gas has filled the ol' barbeque.

Do you get the picture?

When he struck a match and tried to apply the tiny flame to the match-light hole, the over abundant gas that was trapped in the grill, exploded knocking the hat off his head and singeing his eyebrows, not to mention causing him to almost spill what was left of his beer!

This didn't happen to me. My wife pretty much lives by the standard that she does the inside cooking and I do the outside cooking, which includes lighting the grill. But a friend of mine related the aforementioned experience, adding that he thought his wife was pretty damn dumb for leaving the gas on while he was watching a ballgame. I didn't want to get caught up in the middle of a dumb & dumber discussion between a man and his wife, so I jokingly changed the subject.

"Maybe she's not so dumb." I said. "Most of us are worth more dead than we are alive. How much life insurance have you got?"

I was just joking, honest. But he started thinking and told me about how the very next morning after the exploding grill incident, the tube of

BenGay his wife uses for her sore back, got put in the medicine cabinet, "right there where I keep my tube of tooth paste!"

Can you imagine what it would be like to brush your teeth with BenGay? He said it was an experience reminiscent of the time he tried siphoning gas and sucked too long and too hard on the siphon hose. By the time he got done choking, gagging, puking and gasping for air, he had lost all desire to brush his teeth . . . ever again! Besides, the muscles of his gums were so loosened up by the soothing warmth of the BenGay, that it felt like his teeth were going to relax right out of his mouth!

"Well, accidents will happen," I told him. "It's probably nothing to be alarmed about.

"I'll bet the kid's in on it too. He's the one who rubbed the stuff into his mother's back the other day after she complained about twisting her back when she jumped at the sound of the grill exploding." He was on a roll now. "He is probably the one who switched my toothpaste with her BenGay!"

I tried again to calm him. It was a common mistake that happens when you have more than one person with access to the same medicine chest. I told him that my kids never put anything back where it belongs. The same thing could have happened to me a dozen times. (But I usually do look at my toothpaste before I shove it in my mouth. You can never be too careful.)

"But listen to this," he cried. He was getting excited again. "After I got done spitting out all of the BenGay, calling the Poison Control Center, drinking a gallon and a half of milk, and pumping my stomach, I reached into my medicine chest for my Right Guard spray deodorant and gave my underarms a healthy dose. I thought something smelled funny, so I looked at the can and it was my wife's can of Aqua Net hairspray. But since I was gonna be late for work, I just threw a shirt on and took off. Every time I put my arms down at my sides, it felt like I was getting stabbed. That hairspray just about killed me before the day was over!"

I told him that I thought he was over-reacting.

"No, no. You were right! She's out to get me! In 28 years of marriage, she's never lifted one finger to help keep our vehicles in good shape. All she and the kid have ever done is drive 'em and throw their pop cans and trash under the seats." He stopped and looked me square in the eyes, then continued. "When I got home the other night, what do you think she was doing?" he asked. "She was outside actually washing MY car!" he answered, not waiting for my response.

"Don't get anywhere near that car!" I cried. "Don't open the door, throw away your keys and above all, *CANCEL YOUR LIFE INSURANCE!*"

THE INTERNATIONAL TOILET

Since I pay it, I couldn't help but notice that our water bill seemed to jump up pretty high over the last two months. It didn't quite double, but almost. I *hate it* when that happens! I usually can count on my water bill. It is the one constant in my life. It almost always remains the same, within a dollar or two. I know how much to budget for it. And when it almost doubles in size, it really messes up my finances for the month! So when I started whining about the, all of a sudden, high price of water, my wife said that I should quit whining about the water bill and just fix the toilet.

"Fix the toilet? What's wrong with the toilet?" I asked. I had a vision of water spraying all over the bathroom floor! "Is it leaking again?" I could see the living room ceiling slowly turning a dark gray color, and then collapsing all over the carpet and furniture! I could see a massive river of toilet water sluicing down the walls, over my TV and out the window!

"Oh quit being so melodramatic." she said reading my mind again. "I told you about the toilet running all of the time."

Well, it seems as if she might have said something about some sort of a *minor* malfunction with the toilet. Now she informed me that it *runs all of the time*. I personally have never seen our toilet *run*. It doesn't even have legs. It's always just sitting there in the same place when I need it.

"Don't be a smart-ass." She was reading my mind again. (How does she do that?) "Can't you hear it? It runs all night sometimes."

Well, I'm not usually listening for it during the night. (I snore too loud to hear it.) And I'm not usually around to catch it running in the daytime. So I wasn't aware that it was suddenly giving us some disciplinary problems.

"Ooookay, I knew the stool had occasionally been making some funny noises lately." I admitted. The "stool," that's what I call it—my wife calls it the toilet or potty. My mom called it the "can," which is a never ending source of amusement to my wife. Ritzy people call it the commode, which technically is incorrect because a commode was the word used in reference to the little cabinet—usually with legs—that people kept their chamber pot in, back before we had running water enabling us the luxury of a flush toilet.

Things were much simpler when I was a boy. Our family lacked the luxury of running water in one house where we lived. We had an *outhouse* to use in the summer time, but not being overly ritzy people, we used a five gallon bucket for a chamber pot during the cold months. Obviously, no commode was necessary for the five gallon bucket.

Just so you'll know my standing in our home when I was a child. I was the equivalent of that little silver handle you use to flush your toilet with. It was my job to empty the five gallon bucket before school each and every morning. (How's that for an, *I used to walk 5 miles through the snow to school every morning* type of story.)

But anyway, when your stool is running away with your water bill, you really have no choice in the matter except to change the "guts" in the tank to try to get it to slow down. So I got new guts. The other day, I pulled out the directions of how to install the new "guts" in my toilet tank and began to read. (Contrary to popular belief, all men don't look at the directions as a last resort.) The first thing I saw was a stern warning to: *Read ALL Instructions Carefully BEFORE Installing.*

So I immediately commenced to reading those instructions. And I have to admit, they were a might bit confusing at first. In fact, it took me quite a while to read *all* of those instructions *before* I started installation. Oh, I breezed right through the instructions written in English, but I have to admit I struggled with reading the instructions written in Spanish, German, and French.

I had to keep referring back to the English rendition to catch the gist of what the Spanish instructions were saying. And by the time I had done the same with the German instructions, I pretty much had it figured out. So while I looked over the French words, I just compared what I guessed it was saying with the accompanying picture.

First I turned the *agua* off at its source in the basement, and then opened the faucets in the rest of the *haus* to drain the pipes. I ripped out the old "guts" and put in the new in no time flat. Then I went back to the basement to turn the *agua* back on and *Oui* I remembered to turn all of the other faucets back off.

Then, I ran like hell back upstairs to make sure there were no leaks.

Everything looked pretty good. The tank filled and the water shut off, *just like it is suppose to*. I flushed it, waved bye-bye to the swirling water as it disappeared and the tank refilled and the water shut off *just like it is suppose to* again. There was nothing to it.

It was the next morning, during my daily constitutional, just before I had to leave for work, when I heard this curious lapping sound. I looked toward the sound and saw my cat lapping up a little drink from a pool of fresh water on the floor behind the toilet. One of my joints had sprung a leak during the night!

Which instructions had failed me? Spanish? German? French? Naw, I really can't read any of them. And since I can't speak those languages either, I had to rely on good old American English cussing to express my displeasure.

ALIENS

I had a rude awakening a while back. I thought the aliens had landed for sure. When I opened my eyes, it felt like my eyeballs were about to be scalded! Bright light shining in our bedroom window was blinding me! Pain filled my eyeballs and my eyelids plastered themselves shut and refused to open. I didn't know what to do at first. I rolled from side to side and tried to shield them from the light with my pillow.

My mind raced like a thoroughbred on a mile and an eighth track! What to do? If it was aliens out there, I wasn't going to go down easy. I saw the movie "Independence Day!" and I was determined to take as many of them as I could, down with me. I decided that I needed to arm myself first. But my shotguns, rifles and .22 caliber pistol are kept in another room. As are my hunting knives, bow & arrows and my favorite baseball bat.

Quickly in my mind, I surveyed the choice of weapons that I might be able to find closer at hand. Let me think, on the bedside table immediately beside me, there was a picture of my sweet wife, my fireman's pager, my radio alarm clock, car keys, some pocket change, a nasty handkerchief and last but not least, the remote control for our bedroom TV.

Not much to use as a weapon to try to save the world with!

On the other side of the bed, across my sleeping wife from me, was her bedside table. On it, there were a couple of hair brushes, a bottle of Rolaids, a candelabra complete with a eucalyptus scented candle in it, a box of Kleenex, a pen and pad of paper (for listing item numbers of things to order off of QVC), an empty pop can (mine), toenail clippers and a make-up bag (not mine).

Some real lethal stuff there.

I tried opening my eyes again, but the light kept getting brighter and brighter even as I lay there plotting man kinds' defense against these alien intruders. So I knew I was going to have to act fast. They were getting ready to move in!

Once again I tried to open my eyes to get a peek at what they might look like. I thought it might be helpful if I knew how big my adversaries might be. But no dice, the light was just too damn bright!

My dresser is just on the other side of the room. I thought I might have a pocket knife and a couple of belt buckles stashed in the top drawer. If I leaped from bed and made a mad dash to the dresser, would I have time to dig through all of the junk I've accumulated in that drawer and find one of the knives or that one heavy buckle? And say they let me get that far before disintegrating me with a ray gun, would I have time to open the blade and turn to defiantly face them, before their singeing hot rays melted my eye balls to gray glutinous masses? Would I have time to attach the buckle on the end of a belt so I could swing it like a Marine in a bar fight?

Or maybe, since my wife's dresser is closer, I could stop there and fashion a sort of sling shot out of one of her bras (a boyhood fantasy).

Hey, it might work. But then, what would I use for ammunition to shoot at them? Rolaids?

It was about now that I started thinking about my wife laying there peacefully sleeping, totally oblivious to the fate that awaited her. And my daughter and son were also sleeping only a short trip across the hall.

It gave me pause. If it were just me, if I had only myself to worry about, I'd have grabbed the wife's brassiere, attached the ends to a couple of hairbrush handles, loaded the cups up with Rolaids, and let the intruders have it with both barrels!

But, I wasn't in this alone. I had some noncombatants to think about. Maybe I could negotiate a truce. Maybe I could put off their attack long enough for the wife and kids to get out of harm's way. Maybe I could even get them to change their evil, wicked, ways (the aliens I mean). If not, maybe I could at least trick them long enough for me to get into my den and get some real weapons to fight with. Fingernail files and lacy elastic just aren't my style!

My wife rolled over and started mumbling something about good morning to me. She was still asleep, but was struggling to wake up. I was terrified! What if she woke up and made a sudden move?

They could disintegrate her, before she knew what hit her. And there goes the earth. I'd have no chance to even try to save our skins, because if they disintegrated her, there would be hell to pay. I'd be after them like a tom after a kitty-cat in heat! There would be no place they could go. No place they could hide. Nowhere on earth, nowhere in space! I'd follow them to the end of the galaxy! I'd . . .

Before I could finish thinking about what I'd do to them, my wife jumped up out of bed and closed the shade saying,

"That doggone sun sure is bright this morning. You know, you really shouldn't stay up so late watching those science fiction movies. You were babbling about aliens all night."

Well, it's been a long time since I've been in bed late enough to have the sun wake me up.

THE DREAMER

Next Sunday an event will take place that will make many of us forget our troubles and woes. Life will become good again. Our mundane lives will brighten as if the sun has begun to shine again after enduring months of being dark and dreary. The National Football League season begins this Sunday and many of us will walk with a little more spring in our step. We'll feel like kids again.

For football fans, it's kind of like having Christmas come in September. The opening of the NFL season makes many of us start to believe in impossible possibilities: Temperatures will range between 63 degrees at night to a perfect 75 degrees in the day time. The lawnmower will be out of gas, but the cable TV will be in fine working order and the bank will call saying that *they* made a mistake, and your checking account balance isn't overdrawn after all.

You'll step on the scale after a binge of eating and drinking anything and everything that couldn't out run you and you will have *lost* three pounds. Your wife will tell you that she accidentally left steak out to thaw instead of the hamburger she was planning to make meatloaf with for dinner. Your brother-in-law will give back the twenty-five bucks you lent him without you even having to talk to your sister about it.

Beer, pretzels and peanuts will go on sale and your wife will say, "Aw, go ahead, just throw the shells on the floor while you're watching the game. I'll sweep them up later."

You'll call that telephone number that came in the mail saying that all you have to do to win a new boat is call this number . . . and somebody will actually answer!

Your wife will come in the room with a big bowl of popcorn, a cold glass of cola and the remote control and hand all three to you and say, "you decide what we'll watch tonight."

It will be John Wayne night on TBS, Clint Eastwood week on The Movie Channel and there will be a *Gunsmoke* marathon on TV Land.

The catfish will be biting, you will bowl a perfect game and shoot par on the golf course.

Your dog will actually bring you your paper instead of chewing it up, your cats will stop shedding and your kids will actually do their homework.

The spinach crop will fail, the beet crop with fail and chili and crackers will be deemed healthier than broccoli.

The dentist will call and say that your teeth looked so good at your checkup six months ago, that you can just skip the checkup scheduled for Monday.

Your landlord will decide that he has been charging you too much for rent, your neighbor's dog will stop barking and your mosquito bites will quit itching.

The price of gas will drop by thirty-five cents a gallon, natural gas prices will fall and the supply of electricity will grow to record levels.

Your boss will tell you not to worry about being a couple of minutes late in the mornings, you will get an unplanned-for raise and your truck will start getting twenty-five miles to the gallon . . . in town.

Experts will determine that movie popcorn is actually good for you, the telemarketers will lose your phone number and you'll actually get more than one number right on your lottery ticket.

The ragweed crop will fail, the corn market will double and they will find a way to make whole-wheat spaghetti noodles taste good.

The guy squealing his tires in front of your house in the middle of the night will blow one of them, all of the checkout lines will be empty when you're ready to go home and the world will be at peace.

You'll find an extra gallon of milk in your refrigerator, a six-pack of Milky Way candy bars hidden in the Bert & Ernie cookie jar and ice cream will be found to cure cancer.

Your wife will say, "I don't feel like shopping today, let's go fishing." or, "It's your day off, go ahead and go golfing with the guys." or, "Don't worry about that tar you tracked in on my new carpet, it will probably come right out." or, "I think John Wayne is sexy. Let's watch another one of his movies." or, "You've been working way too hard lately. I think you should take a nap." or, "How much money did you want?" or, "You don't have to take me out for dinner, I'll just cook something here at home." or, "You are a *genius!*" or, "You're right *as usual.*" or "You're right *again!*" or even just, "You *are* right."

Bumps in the road will flatten out, ropes set to trip you will fail and as the saying goes, you will be in heaven at least an hour before the devil knows you are dead.

And maybe. . . just maybe, the Minnesota Vikings will win the Super Bowl this year.

BLACKIE AND I

A few years back, my wife and I took in the Star Spangled Spectacular in Storm Lake on July 4th. We got there in time to see part of the parade and then we went to what they called "Artists Alley."

Now, in my opinion, "Artists Alley," is a misnomer. The reason I believe it's been misnamed is obvious. The displays aren't set up in anything close to an alley. They're in one of the nice little lakeside parks that stretch along the north side of Storm Lake. (That is the lake of Storm Lake, not the City of Storm Lake.)

I don't recall the actual name of the park it was held in, but it is the one where they have a cement sidewalk meandering in a loose circuit with several trees planted along the path. At each tree there is a plaque telling a bit of history about the tree. Like, the Buffalo Bill Cottonwood is from a seed from a tree at William Cody's home. And then there's the Colonel Sander's Ash, which came from the Chicken King's Old Kentucky Home. There is even the Moon Tree, grown from an American Sycamore tree seed that accompanied the Apollo 14 astronauts to the moon. It's a neat place. (The park I mean—I've never been to the moon.)

On this particular day, the park was packed. There were hundreds of people walking, well, I don't know if you could actually say they were walking, they were more or less standing around, shuffling their way along the cement path that ran between the artist's booths. And every so often you'd run into a group of "*path blockers*", who were just standing there visiting, seemingly oblivious to the fact that they were holding up the flow of traffic.

Surprisingly, my wife, a woman who walks a twenty minute mile, can melt into a crowd of people like a thin wisp of smoke disappearing in a grove of trees. I started out following her along the path and before I knew it, I had bumped into thirty-seven people while she had slipped through them with about as much friction as gelatin generates sliding off a warm spoon.

I couldn't keep up. But she had on a white sweater and has long brown hair, so I wasn't worried. I could find her. So I watched her bob left, then slide to the right, then right again past one path blocking group after another, while I just kept running into, and almost over, some very grouchy looking women, in my attempt to keep up with her. So finally, I gave up, took my eyes off her white and brown figure as it bobbed and weaved over the horizon and completely out of sight.

No problem, I knew what she was wearing. She shouldn't be too hard to find in this crowd of not more than *two or three thousand* people. I'd just take my time and work around all of these *path blockers* and surely I'd spot a white sweater, with brown hair easy enough.

Do you know how many women that stand about 5-foot 7-inches tall with long brown hair wearing a white sweater there can be in a crowd of two to three thousand? All of them, that's right, damn near every woman down there was dressed exactly like my wife. And, a word to the wise, be careful how you approach a 5-foot 7-inch tall woman with long brown hair wearing a white sweater, just in case it turns out she's not your wife! It's painfully embarrassing when you walk up and give a little pat on the ass to the wrong 5-foot 7-inch tall, long haired woman in a white sweater.

After what seemed like no more than . . . a decade or so, of trying to catch up with her, I got smart. This thing was laid out in a circle, right? And I'd been traveling in the same direction that she was. And she had already proven that she is a better broken field runner than I. So I had no chance of catching up with her by following her. Therefore, in a stroke of genius, I switched my direction and started working backwards around the circle, watching the oncoming crowd for her face. (That is a safer way of recognizing her.)

You know the one thing that amazes me is how many people take their dogs with them everywhere they go. I bet I saw twenty different dogs walking along in that crowd dodging feet. There were so many of us stumblebums stumbling around that they had to be pretty nimble to miss being stepped on.

After what seemed like several hours of searching for my wife going against the grain, I had to stop and take a breather. People kept stepping on past, *brushing on past, pushing on past* and I just kept backing up until I found myself cornered on a small patch of grass with my butt up against the Moon Tree. In front of me there was a group of visiting *path blockers* causing a great road jamb of people, strollers, and even a couple of people in wheel chairs.

I heard a slight whimper and noticed a black Cocker Spaniel tied to one of the *trail blocker's* hands by a leash. He had squirmed away from the crowd, just like me and was rear-ended up against the Moon Tree right beside me.

I looked down at him and he looked up at me. Our eyes met and we bonded - we were both pretty miserable. He whimpered again and the lady with the leash reached down and patted him on the head saying, "All right Blackie, we'll go home now." and she led him off toward the cars.

Lucky dog.

Just about that time, my wife came along and took me by the arm.

"How ya doin'?" she asked.

"I'm ready to go home." I whimpered. And I could have sworn she patted me on the hand and said, "All right, Blackie, we'll go home now," while she led me off toward the car.

Sometimes it's a dog's life.

MR. FIXIT

Got anything around your house that doesn't work? I mean, besides your teenager. I'm talking about something more mechanical, something you bought, paid for, installed and never expected to have to piss with again. Take those little cylinder type door closers. I've got two doors with those closers on them and they worked like they were designed to work for about two . . . maybe even three closes, before they crapped out. You know how they are supposed to work. They allow the door to open to about 90 degrees and when you let go after passing through, instead of the door slamming shut and hitting you in the ass, the cylinder brings it slowly back, with a soft swooshing sound of passing air to gently rest it back on its sill.

Unfortunately, what generally happens is about the third time one of the kids run out of the house, or the wind happens to gust at 50 mph into your newly installed door, or you try to push a 36-inch wide piece of furniture through a 32-inch wide door *without* unhooking the door closer first, the door gets opened farther than 90 degrees. In fact, it gets pushed to . . . oh, say 180 degrees, which does one of two things. Either it bends the push rod in the cylinder so that it will never fit properly inside the cylinder again, or it rips the cylinder from where it is anchored to the door jamb. If the push rod gets bent, the door *may* still close, but it will do so with a spasmodic jerking motion and a series of hesitations which give it the appearance of being confused as to whether it should be closing the door or maybe opening it again.

If it rips loose from the door jamb, it's a fairly easy fix . . . the first time. You can just move its anchor point up or down about an inch and screw it back into the wood again. But you are pretty much limited to two fixes this way one move up and one move down. You move it any farther than that, and you end up bending the cylinder yourself and you have little recourse but to install a new one.

In either case, you've got an addition to your "Honey do" list to help fill all of that spare time that you would otherwise be wasting on the golf course or at your favorite fishing hole. To be honest, I've pretty successfully ignored the door closer problems at our house. One door doesn't get used much and we've more or less gotten used to the other one flopping around either opening or closing. We're never quite sure which.

But I've got one fixit project I don't think the wife is going to forget about. Our kitchen light keeps blowing its bulb. It doesn't sound like too big of a deal, but, the wife keeps mumbling something about "trying to cook in the dark" in a disparaging manner and the kids keep whining about not being able to see when they go into the kitchen at night.

I don't see what the big problem is. I mean, what do they think the lights in the refrigerator, microwave oven and range hood are for? Just open the fridge and micro doors and push the range hood light on and if you want to see the floor, turn on the oven light.

What's the problem? But these modern housewives . . . we've got them spoiled. She seems to think that just because electricity is available, we should have a regular light in the kitchen. Go figure. But this time it looks like I'm going to have to break down and fix it. For all the grief I've been catching over this light thing, you'd think it was something important, like the TV that wasn't working.

A NEW DOOR

Every spring and summer since we moved into our house, when the humidity gets high, the wife and I have been fighting with a sticking door. The door had a tendency to swell up from the humidity and stick. Sometimes it would stick so tight we didn't even need to lock it at night. A robber would need more than burglary tools to get it open. It would have taken a sledge hammer to break it open. (But I didn't, I promise.)

Why didn't I just cut it off a little? Because in the winter time when the air is cold and dry, the door shrinks back down to let a nice draft of cold air waft into the house so I didn't think cutting it off was the answer.

Replacing it was . . . I thought.

I don't hate all doors. It's just the ones that I have to install. I spent a three-day weekend, last weekend putting a new door in our house. My god, what a job! I had fun tearing the old door out. I like tearing things apart and I'm told that I'm good at it. I tried to be careful and not break anything while tearing the old door out, just in case something happened and I had to put it back in. But I had to do some sawing and beating with a hammer (my favorite cordless tool) that rendered the old door unusable before it was all said and done. At that point, it became an onward and upward task with no turning back, no changing of the mind and no room for weak-kneed hesitancy. (A little less nagging would have been nice though.)

I do admit to a certain feeling of trepidation after the door removal. After all, I had just attacked a portion of the superstructure of our home with a reciprocating saw and a 16 ounce fiberglass handled hammer. Consequently, when my wife ended that first day's labor with an insistent request that we go to Wal-Mart, I was hesitant to go because I had just produced a huge open hole in the north side of our house.

Sidebar: My wife will not normally leave our house without locking it up tight. I suppose the reason for this stems back to when we were dating, before we were married, I left my doors unlocked all the time and one night, some punks opened my unlocked door, walked in and stole all of my cassette tapes. I think the loss of those tapes ingrained upon her mind a certain fear of losing personal possessions and how important locking your doors is when it comes to non-professional thieves who will steal things of no real value. (We don't have anything valuable enough for professional thieves to waste their time on.)

But when it came to risking our possessions by leaving a big hole in the house for an extended trip to Wal-Mart, she was willing to take the chance. So that night, we had only a thin layer of plastic that I tacked across the door to keep out the thieves and the flies and the evil, West Nile Virus-carrying mosquitoes.

Sidebar over—back to the door installation.

You know, I didn't really have much trouble ripping down the plastic the next day and setting the new door into the hole. The new door was a steel door that was already framed up. So all I had to do is make the hole the right size to set it in and make it square enough for the door to function. (That is to make it so it will open *and* close without the use of a sledge hammer or crowbar.)

The first problem of the day was reconstructing a new door sill. (Somewhere between the reciprocating sawing and the hammering, the old door sill kinda got ruined along with a little of the foundation.)

Constructing a new sill took me a while and by the time I got the sill good and solid (and level) and had began cutting boards for the jamb, the wife needed me to take her out for a sandwich for dinner and of course, a short trip to Wal-Mart for something we had forgotten the night before. When I balked, she complained that "you never want to go to Wal-Mart with me."

Once again, we left, leaving a gapping hole in the north side of our house.

It was a relatively quick trip, (we left at 10:30 a.m.) by 3:00 p.m., I was hard at the door again and by 8:00 p.m. I had actually set the door in place and framed it up on the outside of the house. I went to bed that night secure in the knowledge that any intruder, except for flies and mosquitoes, would have to at least, pull the door open, to gain entrance. (I hadn't installed the latch or lock yet and there were a couple of holes for winged intruders to pass through.)

Here-in lies the reason for my true hatred of door installation. I actually like the cutting and hammering involved in tearing out old doors. I even enjoyed the hammering in, and the framing-up parts of setting the new door in place. But installing that stupid hardware drives me wild! Sticking the handle on one side and a knob on the other side of the door and lining the two up so that the stupid screws that hold the goddamn thing together, would try the patients of a saint! And a saint, I am not!

I would like to use this forum to apologize to my neighbors, friends and anyone within a seventeen mile radius who probably could hear my cursing as I labored away the day trying to merely put a knob and lock on that frigging door. First I couldn't get the screws to line up. And then when I did, the lock lever had become disengaged and nothing worked. Then, I got it together so the lock would work with the key, but not with the lock lever, or it would work with the lock lever, but the key wouldn't work. Then the key got stuck and wouldn't come out. Then, the key came out, but wouldn't go back in!

I was about to fix the whole thing using my favorite cordless tool, when my wife suggested a quick trip to Wal-Mart. And to show you the state I was in . . . I actually wanted to go!

HOUSING THE HOMELESS

It's been brought to my attention recently that there has been a great influx of homeless individuals who have immigrated to this area. It is a problem that has plagued many other parts of the country for a long time now. How these homeless immigrants will affect the social and cultural lives of those of us with homes is, as yet, an unanswered question.

But they are here, so we have to find a way to cope with them. Many people in this area have already started. They have taken the initiative, on their own, with no government interference, to begin providing these homeless migrants with clean, affordable housing. They have either built them houses with their own hands or bought them houses and moved them into their own back and front yards, where they erect them for all to see.

But as far as I can see, the jury is still out as to whether their efforts are appreciated by the ones the housing is meant for. I see a lot of these individuals floating around the area with no apparent aim in life. They don't even seem to be too interested in the housing that is being offered to them free of charge! In fact, it is really hard to see if they even use these nice homes. I can't say I've even seen a single individual going into, or coming out of one of the houses. That's why I've been dragging my feet every time my wife starts nagging at me to buy or build a *butterfly house* to put out in our yard.

I mean why should I go to all of the cost and effort to provide a bunch of lazy butterflies with a house to live in? I ask you, why? If they want a house, let them build their own. I mean, can you imagine what kind of care a butterfly would take of a house. You couldn't depend on them to fix anything that went wrong with it.

"A butterfly can't fix that loose board. Their hands are too small to pick up the hammer. They can't be expected to mow their share of the lawn. Insects aren't strong enough to push the mower."

Yeah right, excuses, excuses. Those butterflies are a lazy bunch anyway. I've never known one to have a job, let alone hold one long enough to earn enough money to pay rent. All they want to do is float around on the summer breeze and look pretty. All the while, they are actually on a devious mission to steal the nectar right out of our flowering plants!

So what do we do? We run right out and buy houses for them and stick them up out in our yards. Nine times out of ten, they just ignore them anyway, the ungrateful buggers. So far, I've fought off my wife's arguments to buy one. She says if we put a house up for them, it might attract all kinds of butterflies to our area. Oh, sure, then you've opened yourself up for all kinds of social and cultural problems. You'd have orange ones, and yellow ones, or white ones, some with a touch of a green or blue tint. She seems to think that Monarchs and Swallowtails would have no problems coexisting. But I happen to know that if you encourage a bunch of different kinds of butterflies to overrun a back yard, sooner or later, the moths are going to move in too and, well, there goes the neighborhood.

And then the other day she decided that the birds in our neighborhood are dirty! Yeah that's right, we've got *dirty birds*! What do you do when your birds are dirty? I guess you buy them a bird bath. That's what my wife did anyway!

There it is, sitting out in our yard all white and shining. It's filled with tepid rain water, just waiting for the birds to come and take a bath. But I don't think those birds are too interested in personal hygiene because I haven't seen one glide in, strip down and dive in yet. And I've been watching because we've got some pretty good looking chickadees that hang out around our house.

But I suppose it's just as well our bath doesn't become too popular. You know how things are when word gets out about a new hot spot to cool off. Before long there will probably be an overcrowding problem and I'll end up hiring a lifeguard. Then there's always some who would sneak back to the bath at night and before we know it, there'll be a wild bird orgy going on. And if somebody slips and falls and breaks a leg or a wing . . . I'll be liable. After all, I invited them onto my property by placing the bath there in the first place. If I didn't provide them with a safe place and guard it sufficiently after hours, it'll be the same as my fault. And I don't know if my homeowners insurance will cover birdbath accidents or not! You've got to be careful when you are considering lawn ornamentation.

Now the wife is looking at a couple of new items. She's made eyes at a little stone turtle and mentioned that she saw the cutest little cement skunk! My God, what if one of the neighbors gets sprayed!

THE ENTREPRENEUR

Just who the heck is responsible for Valentine's Day anyway? According to my American Heritage Talking Dictionary computer disk, it could have been some guy named Saint Valentine. He was a Roman Christian who was martyred during the persecution of Christians by Emperor Claudius II. Or it could have been this other guy named Valentine, who was also martyred. This guy was the Bishop of Terni, which is a region of present day central Italy. If one of these guys is actually responsible for what we now call Valentine's Day, maybe that's why ol' Claud was persecuting them. He didn't want to buy his wife a gift every February 14th. So, he figured, I'll just torture these jerks and they'll forget this nonsense. If that's the case, his plan didn't work.

But then, the dictionary went on to say that another guy, named Geoffrey Chaucer might be the guy responsible for the big deal our wives make out of Valentine's Day. It said that somewhere around the year, 1380, this Chaucer guy composed something he called *Parlement of Foules*. In it, he wrote something like, *"Seynt (Saint) Valentine's Day, When every foul cometh there to chese [choose] his make [mate]."*

The whole thing sounds kind of fishy to me. The guy couldn't spell a lick. How did they derive at the idea that I should buy my wife something (preferably with diamonds on it) every February 14th, from some little ditty about chickens (he wrote *foul*, but probably meant fowl.) written over six hundred years ago? And how on earth did it actually catch on here in America? Are we nuts?

I'll tell you what. It wasn't Saint Valentine or Bishop Valentine or even good old Jeff Chaucer that hung this on us modern day Americans. It might surprise you to know that it wasn't even our wives or our lovers (for me they're one of the same) who placed this expensive little holiday on our bent backs. They're just trying to cash in on it.

I have to say that it is our own government that is responsible for Valentine's Day being the fiasco that it is. No, I'm not trying to pin something else on the President. What I mean to say is our *form* of government is to blame. It is a republic with democratic principles that supports a Free Enterprise system.

That is the crux of the matter. We are a nation of entrepreneurs who utilize the Free Enterprise idea to the fullest. The Greeting Card Industry makes a mint selling Valentines. The candy companies make a bigger mint selling candy to children and adults. It's a huge time of year for flower shops and jewelry stores offering bouquets of fragrant flowers and diamond rings, bracelets and necklaces guaranteed to melt the object of a man's desire's heart. And then there's the grocery stores offering chocolate, peanuts and beer as a suitable gift for the male half of the equation.

So we have only our own good life, to blame for the hassle of yet another holiday requiring the purchase of a gift for our wives or girl friends. (Preferably not both.) There is a virtual fortune to be acquired with the right idea.

I'm certainly not averse to using the entrepreneurial spirit to make myself rich by cashing in on Valentine's Day. So, I've come up with an idea designed to help out you guys who either forgot that Valentine's Day is a gift giving holiday or were too cheap to fork over the bucks required to buy your sweetie a gift.

You can spend $15 or $20 bucks on just flowers and candy, easy. You can spend a couple of hundred if you're not careful and start looking at jewelry. But I have a money saving solution for you.

It's really simple. All you need is *A Good Excuse*! That's where I come in. You tell me how big of an excuse you need and I'll charge you accordingly. My basic standard excuse will cost you only $5. But the big one, the fool proof, "Golly I can't afford to buy her that diamond ring, but I still want to get in her pants" excuse will run you a little more. The total cost depends upon just how much you are trying to save.

Examples would be: $5—*Aw shucks, I knew there was something I was forgetting. I'll catch you next year.* $10—*Gosh Baby, on the way to buy your Valentine's gift I blew the engine in my car. It cost all the money I had to get it fixed, just so I could drive over here to be with you. I'm sorry!* $20 & Up—*I bought a ring and a whole dozen red roses for you, Babe. But on the way up here, these five big guys jumped me! I fought like a wild tiger, but in the end, they overpowered me and took your ring and the flowers. I can live with my bruises, my cuts, scratches, and broken bones, but baby, I can't live if you won't tell me you forgive me for being too whimpy to protect your gift from those five big desperate flower thieves!*

Cuts, bruises, and black eyes are all included. These excuses are practically guaranteed to work like a charm and I got a million of 'em, so you can give me a call next year too!

THE OPTIMIST

Recently, my wife had a complaint about me! I know that's hard to believe. But I guess it's hard to be perfect, so I'll just have to accept the fact that there is something about me that she doesn't like so well.

She said that she thinks I *"get angry too often."* Now where she got that idea, I'll never know. When questioned, all she could say was something about how she doesn't like it when I stomp my foot, curse loudly and exhibit a general tendency to throw things.

Hey, wait a minute. That's not me. I'll not deny that I've been known to throw a hammer after striking my thumb with it. And admittedly, the names that I called it probably could have been termed a form of cursing. But I don't *ever* remember stomping my foot.

I will admit that occasionally, well, maybe quite often even, I do express my unhappiness about certain situations with actions that *could* be construed as my being angry, but not without good reason. I think that I get mad so often because I am an optimist. You may think it is odd that a person should blame a flaw in his character on optimism, but if you listen to what I have to say, you might agree with me.

I can pretty much credit my constantly running battle with inanimate objects for *most* of my anger tantrums. There is nothing and I mean *nothing* that can set me off as fast as some non-living, non-breathing, non-seeing, hearing or moving object that gets in my way or causes me a bunch of grief. And I really feel that this attitude stems almost totally from my optimistic attitude on life.

How, you may ask, can being optimistic about life make a person mad? Let's analyze pessimism to find out our answer. A pessimist enters a dark room *expecting* to bang his (or her) shin on the coffee table. An optimist, on the other hand, enters that same dark room not *expecting* to bang his shin on the coffee table. So, when the pessimist enters the dark room, bangs his shin on the coffee table, it's not totally unexpected. Therefore when it happens, the pessimist merely says:

"I knew it! I just knew I was going to bang my shins on that stupid, son-of-a-gun coffee table."

But when an optimist enters the dark room and bangs his shin on that damn coffee table, it is a complete and total surprise! And let's face it, surprises that are not only complete and total, but painful too, really tend to piss an optimist off because he doesn't expect bad things to happen! Therefore, when it happens, the optimist says something angry like, "YOU DIRTY ROTTEN SON-OF-A-BITCHIN' BASTARD" and turns the coffee table into kindling.

A pessimist is also not surprised when his pen falls out of his shirt pocket as he bends over to tie his shoes. He wakes up expecting every bad thing that can possibly happen to happen. So if the worst thing that happens to him all day is that his pen falls out of his shirt pocket as he bends over to tie his shoes, it's no big deal. Heck, he's probably glad the dang pen fell out of his pocket! He's probably happy to scramble around looking for it! It's probably the high point of his whole day!

But that is not how an optimist works. He wakes up thinking only good thoughts. He expects only good things will happen. That's why he is ill-prepared to accept as a natural act, that his pen falls from his pocket *every fucking time* he bends over to tie his *fucking* shoes. That's when he reduces the pen to a shattered pile of smashed plastic and ink! (I think I just figured out where she got that part about stomping my foot.)

And while my optimism shows most when dealing with inanimate objects, another observation I might note is that when a pessimist walks into his house and steps on his favorite cat's tail, he is not surprised, because, once again, "a pessimist is always looking for the worst thing to happen."

Unlike the optimist who expects the best to happen, which in this case would be that the stupid cat, being a living, breathing, hearing, and seeing creature, would see or hear him coming and move the hell out of the way!

Now when the pessimist steps on the cat, even though it yowls, it's no great surprise and the pessimist jumps back and the cat runs off with only a slight kink in his tail. But when the optimist steps on his cat's tail, its screech scares the living shit out of him and he pivots to run. The cat, who obviously isn't crazy about some guy who weighs an eighth of a ton pivoting on his tail, decides that it might be an opportune time to get even with the optimist for neutering him and buries his claws in the optimist's upper thigh! What can I say? The optimist does the instinctive thing . . . kicks hell out of the cat! All of which gets the optimist in trouble with both his wife and his daughter.

I've tried to be more pessimistic about life. I've tried getting up in the morning and wondering what terrible thing will happen to me today, just so I'll be ready for it and not be surprised so I don't have to get angry quite so often. But I have trouble with that. I guess it's because most pessimists whom I know, are pretty unhappy people. If I can have my druthers, I'd rather be happy, than unhappy.

So, I just keep stumbling through life, looking for the good things to happen even though it means getting a little mad once in a while. I guess I'm just cursed with optimism.

OPPOSITES

I went to church last Sunday. (Don't worry, the roof didn't cave in.) I'll admit that I don't attend every Sunday, but, the wife and I do go on special occasions such as Christmas and Easter and whenever our grandkids are singing with the rest of the Sunday school kids.

I'm not writing this to make excuses for not attending regularly or to justify my place in heaven just because I go to church to celebrate the birth and resurrection of Christ and when my grandkids are performing. I write this to share with you the quiet feeling of contentment that I felt as my grandchildren came down off the stage and filtered into the pews to join their parents and my wife and I, after they were done singing.

Don't get me wrong. I claim no credit for the fact that our children have chosen to have their children attend Sunday school. But, I take great pride in our kids for the fact that they do take the time and make the effort to have their children take part in Sunday school.

The feeling that came over me when the little guys came tripping into the pews Sunday morning reminded me of the segment of CBS Sunday Morning I had watched shortly before we walked over to the church.

The segment was about one of those computer dating services that are always promising to help bring lonely single persons together. The particular one they were covering on Sunday Morning was the one that says they ask people 500 questions which helps them to develop a "Personality Profile" for each person which leads to uniting only people who are totally compatible.

The guy doing the interview asked the computer dating service guy, "What about opposites attracting?" The dating service guy answered that, "Opposites attracting opposites is a recipe for disaster."

At the time, I remember thinking that might have been a reasonable statement. But, when I looked over at my wife in church Sunday, as two of the boys slipped right past me and went to their grandma, one sitting on her lap and the other, snuggling in close, under her arm to lay his head up against her side I thought of what that guy had said. And as I watched this unabridged scene of unfettered affection unfold before my eyes, all I could think was, *was that guy full of shit or what.*

I thought that, because two more opposite people than what my wife and I are, do not exist on this earth. How are we opposite? I don't know if I have enough time, or space to list all the ways we are opposite. In fact I know I don't. But I can list some of the more obvious.

I love to watch football. She hates to watch football. I love to watch college basketball. She hates to watch college basketball. I hate spinach. She likes it. I like to go on fishing trips. She'd rather I didn't. I like new, fuel-efficient automobiles. She likes old, classic, gas guzzling race cars. She likes to watch music videos. I refuse to watch music videos. She likes long hair on men. I like long hair on women. She says my eyes are green. I say they are blue.

She likes to shop. I don't. She likes beef better than pork. I like pork better than beef. She likes chicken on her pizza. I don't understand why? She's a perfectionist. I'm a slob. She reads magazines, *while* we watch a movie. (That really bugs me.) She likes light-hearted comedies. I like action adventures. She likes the volume low. I like it loud. She likes oatmeal and coconut. I only like them if they are together with chocolate chips . . . in cookie form.

My wife doesn't curse. I do. Conversely, she thinks that when comedians like George Carlin or Eddie Murphy curse, they are just being cute. But when I curse when I'm angry, I'm a bad guy. I don't agree.

She hates it when I have control of the remote. I hate it when she has control of the remote. Consequently, she watches television upstairs and I watch television downstairs.

She chooses who to vote for by who looks more *presidential.* I listen to what they have to say and vote for the person with whom I best agree with.

She thinks that every day on the calendar that is denoted in red, is a gift-giving holiday. I think gifts on Christ's birth, your own birth, and Mother's Day are enough.

I could go on and on, but that is probably enough and I'd hate to bore you. But what I'm trying to say here is that as I watched my wife with our grandsons Sunday, it dawned on me that a successful relationship can't just depend upon complete compatibility. If it did, we would have been doomed from the start and Sunday's scene wouldn't have happened. I think a successful relationship depends more upon what is inside people and how willing you are to give and take and compromise, not taking life too seriously and having a sense of humor. An example would be when she mentioned to me the other day, that our next anniversary will be our 36th. (*Thirty-six years* with the same old woman!)

"Is that a big deal?" I asked.

"Big enough that you should mark it on your calendar" she said, adding, ". . . *in red*."

THE END

DISCLAIMER: While this memoir is published as nonfiction, I must admit to using a certain amount of "poetic license," including some extemporaneous descriptions of events that may or may not have actually happened along with a few gross exaggerations. And in light of this revelation, I would like to ask that you not tell my wife about its existence.

Thank you.
Roger Stoner

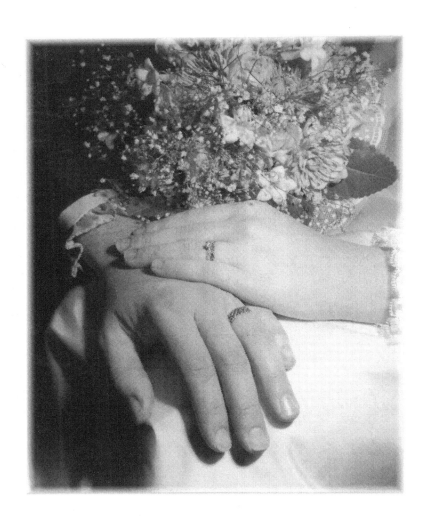

93954509R00110

Made in the USA
Lexington, KY
21 July 2018